Exemplifying Contemporary Challenges in Global Politics and Societies

Edited by Izabela A. Dahl

Published in London, United Kingdom

Exemplifying Contemporary Challenges in Global Politics and Societies
http://dx.doi.org/10.5772/intechopen.1004489
Edited by Izabela A. Dahl

Contributors
Glenn Wasson, Izabela A. Dahl, Mara Santi, Stella Micheong Cheong, Tihomir Cipek

© The Editor(s) and the Author(s) 2025

The rights of the editor(s) and the author(s) have been asserted in accordance with the Copyright, Designs and Patents Act 1988. All rights to the book as a whole are reserved by INTECHOPEN LIMITED. The book as a whole (compilation) cannot be reproduced, distributed or used for commercial or non-commercial purposes without INTECHOPEN LIMITED's written permission. Enquiries concerning the use of the book should be directed to INTECHOPEN LIMITED rights and permissions department (permissions@intechopen.com).

Violations are liable to prosecution under the governing Copyright Law.

Individual chapters of this publication are distributed under the terms of the Creative Commons Attribution 4.0 License which permits commercial use, distribution and reproduction of the individual chapters, provided the original author(s) and source publication are appropriately acknowledged. If so indicated, certain images may not be included under the Creative Commons license. In such cases users will need to obtain permission from the license holder to reproduce the material. More details and guidelines concerning content reuse and adaptation can be found at http://www.intechopen.com/copyright-policy.html.

Notice

Statements and opinions expressed in the chapters are these of the individual contributors and not necessarily those of the editors or publisher. No responsibility is accepted for the accuracy of information contained in the published chapters. The publisher assumes no responsibility for any damage or injury to persons or property arising out of the use of any materials, instructions, methods or ideas contained in the book.

First published in London, United Kingdom, 2025 by IntechOpen
IntechOpen is the global imprint of INTECHOPEN LIMITED, registered in England and Wales, registration number: 11086078, 167-169 Great Portland Street, London, W1W 5PF, United Kingdom

For EU product safety concerns: IN TECH d.o.o., Prolaz Marije Krucifikse Kozulić 3, 51000 Rijeka, Croatia, info@intechopen.com or visit our website at intechopen.com.

British Library Cataloguing-in-Publication Data
A catalogue record for this book is available from the British Library

Exemplifying Contemporary Challenges in Global Politics and Societies
Edited by Izabela A. Dahl
p. cm.
Print ISBN 978-0-85014-883-1
Online ISBN 978-0-85014-882-4
eBook (PDF) ISBN 978-0-85014-884-8

If disposing of this product, please recycle the paper responsibly.

IntechOpen

intechopen.com

Built by scientists, for scientists

Explore all IntechOpen books

Meet the editor

Izabela A. Dahl is an associate professor and senior lecturer in history, focusing on gender and intercultural relations. Her main research interests include modern and contemporary European history. Her projects cover migration and refugee studies, relief efforts, the history of anti-Semitism, Jewish history, European memory culture, and international relations in the Baltic Sea region, with a particular focus on democratization processes. Her analysis is driven by an interest in social power structures and dynamics that influence cultural and social contexts. Her work is epistemologically shaped by discourse analysis, intersectionality, narrativity, oral sources in historical writing, and source pluralism. In her empirical research, she often employs approaches that examine gender dynamics, social inclusion and exclusion processes, and social categorization.

Contents

Preface — IX

Chapter 1 — 1
Introductory Chapter: Exemplifying Contemporary Challenges in Global Politics and Society
by Izabela A. Dahl

Chapter 2 — 9
Conservative Revolution and Nationalism
by Tihomir Cipek

Chapter 3 — 25
Globalization: Challenges and Effects on Europe Post-WWII
by Izabela A. Dahl

Chapter 4 — 43
Perspective Chapter: Brexit, Emmanuel Macron and the Resurgence of the *Europe puissance*
by Glenn Wasson

Chapter 5 — 59
A Tale of Two Cities: Navigating the Politics of Hate of North Korean Migrants in Seoul and New Malden
by Stella Micheong Cheong

Chapter 6 — 81
Perspective Chapter: The Illusion of Dystopian Justice as a Means toward Social Justice. K-drama's Global Success Unveiled
by Mara Santi

Preface

The volume *Exemplifying Contemporary Challenges in Global Politics and Societies* addresses complex factors shaping today's global environment. It examines how ideas, goods, and people circulate amid political fragmentation and societal shifts, while also addressing inequalities and the adjustments of traditional social structures in response to changing social conditions. Concerning the rise of populism and political polarization, the anthology explores the conditions and implications of these phenomena, linking them to historically dynamic processes characterized by disruptions, shifts, and continuities. The contributions provide examples of the evolving dynamics of global interconnectedness, analyzing its political and social ramifications. Drawing on the dynamics of migration, the book offers examples of the multifaceted nature of societal mobility and its impact on cultural assimilation experiences. It unpacks the complexities of social and political disruptions in an increasingly interconnected world, shedding light on the agency exercised by individuals.

The contribution of this volume lies in providing interdisciplinary analytical nuance into the currently challenged and re-signified globalization, outlining challenges of governance amidst increasing polarization, exemplifying the complexities of integration and coalition-building against the erosion of democratic norms. By doing so, the contributions do not separate the matter from the idea, offering a comprehensive approach to global issues concisely.

In addition to the "Introductory Chapter: Exemplifying Contemporary Challenges in Global Politics and Society", which identifies the main contributions of global perspectives and advocates for employing interdisciplinary approaches in studies of contemporary global issues, the volume comprises five other chapters that approach and exemplify global issues from various disciplinary angles. The volume combines contributions on political and historical ideas that remain highly relevant to modern liberal democracies amid the rise of nationalist rhetoric in liberal contexts, with contributions on social injustice that point to the limitations of liberal democracies as communicated through popular culture.

In chapter 2, "Conservative Revolution and Nationalism", Tihomir Cipek traces back to the early 20th century, exploring the history of political ideas with a focus on the conservative revolution. Cipek discusses the emergence of the term 'Conservative Revolution' as a battle for values linked to national identity and expressed through culture. Drawing on several key texts written by prominent writers and cultural figures of the time, the author evaluates the utopian aspects of the conservative revolution that continue to attract the right. Applying discourse analysis, the chapter examines language and thought as components of national identity, questioning the nation's relationship with the West. The ideas of the conservative revolution reveal the limits of the liberal interpretation of lifeworld, which is why the thinkers of the conservative revolution concerned themselves with language, myth, religion, and national identity. Cipek's contribution explores the link between language and the nation's 'spirit', analyzing how war is viewed as the highest achievement of national history and discussing the idea that liberalism cannot align with a nation's "true" values. Additionally, it examines the views of conservative revolutionaries on the West and Russia.

In chapter 3, "Globalization: Challenges and Effects on Europe Post-WWII", Izabela A. Dahl analyzes Europe's integration during the Cold War. Drawing from a review of current knowledge about the Cold War, Dahl summarizes the political and economic development paths of Western and Eastern Europe before the Soviet Union's fall. She argues that, despite the divergent paths in the East and West toward twentieth-century neoliberal democratic models, some commonalities related to the shared need for welfare can be identified beyond the political and ideological divide in Europe. This chapter investigates the causes, challenges, and impacts of European globalization, emphasizing the key economic, political, and social factors shaping this process.

Glenn Wasson, in chapter 4 titled "Perspective Chapter: Brexit, Emmanuel Macron and the Resurgence of the *Europe puissance*", provides an example of how the concept of 'Europe puissance' helps identify divisions among EU partners when NATO became Europe's voice in geopolitical matters. The focus is on recent tensions in European politics, including Brexit and Macron's revived idea of a unified European military force for collective defence. Drawing on the term 'Europe puissance', which describes European power as strategic autonomy and sovereignty, following the tradition of General de Gaulle in the early 1960s, Wasson shows that one of France's main political goals is to establish a unified defense policy among its partners, and within the scope of an expanded partnership since 2017 that includes a broader Euro-Atlantic community. Wasson argues that due to historical continuities, although Brexit allowed Macron to boost France's leadership in Europe, the 'Europe puissance' idea faced similar challenges as before – specifically, the desire for Europe to reduce dependence on the United States, and the lack of a supranational structure, which historically hindered Franco-German relations during Ludwig Wilhelm Erhard's presidency.

The last two chapters of the volume address issues of social injustice and unrest caused by democratic systems failing to ensure social equity. Stella Micheong Cheong, in chapter 5 titled "A Tale of Two Cities: Navigating the Politics of Hate of North Korean Migrants in Seoul and New Malden", uses autobiographical narrative inquiries and provides an analysis of the concept of 'bridging civic identities', characterized by cosmopolitanism, interconnectedness, and imagination, enabling the transformation of conflict-driven civic identities into peacebuilding civic identities. Micheong Cheong explores personal experiences of migrants by examining how North Korean migrants in Seoul and New Malden navigate their path toward integration and civic identity, highlighting the role of hate politics. Micheong Cheong illustrates how migrants maintain remarkable resilience against structural and personal forms of oppression and how they develop a unique identity that links their heritage with their new lives. In this way, the chapter offers an example of how North Korean migrants can become 'bridge citizens'—individuals who not only overcome hate-driven politics but also help foster social cohesion and peace within their communities.

The last chapter of the volume, chapter 6 by Mara Santi, "Perspective Chapter: The Illusion of Dystopian Justice as a Means toward Social Justice. K-drama's Global

Success Unveiled", focuses on the depiction of social hardship and the struggle of the powerless in neoliberal democracies in K-dramas. The study demonstrates how Korean TV series have become a transnational phenomenon by exploring issues of worldwide relevance.

Izabela A. Dahl
The Institute of Contemporary History,
Södertörn University,
Stockholm, Sweden

Chapter 1

Introductory Chapter: Exemplifying Contemporary Challenges in Global Politics and Society

Izabela A. Dahl

1. Introduction

In times when global strategic power relations are being revised, security threats increase alongside social uncertainty and inequality. During these periods, contributions that explore the changing dynamics of global interconnectedness, analyzing their political and social ramifications, not least from a historical perspective, are essential to identify the issues, discuss their various aspects, present ongoing research reflecting these changes, and support potential solutions. These efforts are vital because they encourage looking both backward and forward in time.

The introductory chapter addresses the shift in popular understanding of globalization that fuels the current discussions on the topic. It provides an overview of the key findings in knowledge surrounding contemporary studies of global issues and advocates for interdisciplinary exchange involving multidisciplinary approaches to empirically exemplify global issues, thereby mobilizing academic discussions on the complex nature of global processes.

2. The interpretational shift of globalization as a concept

Over the last 35 years, the world has undergone a significant shift in how the term "globalization" is commonly used. Since the 1990s, globalization has become a buzzword in both research and public debates, capturing the profound changes brought about by political, economic, and technological transformations. In 1998, the United Nations Secretary Kofi Annan phrased the then-popular meaning of the term: "Globalization is commonly understood to describe the advances in technology and communications that have made possible an unprecedented degree of financial and economic interdependence and growth. As markets are integrated, investments flow more easily, competition is enhanced, prices are lowered, and the living standards everywhere are improved" [1].

The historical circumstances, including the collapse of the Soviet bloc and the end of the Cold War, particularly with the fall of the Berlin Wall, which eliminated the distinction between the communist and capitalist worlds in Europe, also fueled the debate on "globalization." The beginning of transformation altered the common understanding of the term "globalization," highlighting that the world and its people were now a single entity rather than divided spheres of ideologies and superpower interests. In this sense, "globalization" could imply that the world is coming together [2].

The optimistic tone of the imagined integration reflected how corporate and political elites embraced transnational flows of goods, services, capital, and ideas as the new forces driving social progress. In this context, Manuel Castell used the term "globalization" to describe a form of capitalism built on global networks that expanded in the 1990s. Geographical divisions and political boundaries became less important in the new economy enabled by advanced communication technologies, and Castell argued that the new generation of information society was creating new centers and peripheries that did not follow the borders of nation-states [3].

The concept of nation-states was also challenged in academic research by new, emerging interdisciplinary academic fields within the social sciences. As Manfred B. Steger and Paul James argue, a new wave of scholarship understood that fully unlocking globalization as a field of study required two major academic shifts: extending and reconfiguring traditional disciplinary approaches to social analysis and moving beyond the dominant framework of international relations [4–6]. The new field of global studies challenged the traditional impact of "methodological nationalism" by questioning the treatment of the nation-state as the default unit of analysis. Although scholars often debated the specific details and effects of globalization, there was a broad consensus that a new global era was beginning. The term "globalization" came to evoke a sense of inevitability and irreversibility, reinforcing the idea that the course of social change was already set.

Within the globalization discourse of the 1990s, two slogans—"the end of history" and "the war of civilizations"—were highlighted, the first by Francis Fukuyama and the second by Samuel P. Huntington. In his book "The End of History and the Last Man" (1992), Fukuyama argued that the coming age was characterized by the "end of history": after a period in which radically different societal orders competed, one had prevailed. The market-based liberal democracy remained a universal model for world civilization. The unique ability of the market and democracy to generate economic prosperity while fulfilling people's needs for recognition and equal influence has made liberal democracy a dominant and universal form of governmental model. A global world civilization was emerging from this foundation. Billions of ordinary people around the world fell for the neoliberal temptation, confident that they, too, would soon reap the material benefits of market globalization.

Against Fukuyama's relatively optimistic view regarding the establishment of the liberal order stood Huntington's more pessimistic one in his book "The Clash of Civilizations and the Remaking of the World Order" (1997). Huntington put forward the argument that although technological achievements had a global impact, everyone had to accept modern advancements in this area, which did not necessarily mean that shared moral, political, or cultural values were being established. Conversely, as the world became more interconnected and therefore smaller, conflicts between cultures would intensify, and confrontations would become more inevitable as proximity breeds sharper antagonism. Non-Western civilizations would strive to assert their identity by increasingly distancing themselves from everything Western and from each other. Following Huntington, the most educated would lead this identity struggle, which would soon manifest as terrorism and armed conflict. He argued that the rise of the information society and new communication technologies had not led to a more unified or peaceful world. Instead, it has increased division and conflict. Rather than easing differences, communication often highlights and intensifies them. The core cultural differences become even more apparent within this new global landscape.

Huntington's critical perspective on the ongoing global development was not only validated already by the al-Qaeda terrorist attack against the United States, but as Manfred B. Steger and Paul James emphasize, within just 20 years, the concept of "globalization" evolved into a political scapegoat used by the rising national populist movements on both the right and left worldwide [4, 7–10]. The so-called "irrational exuberance" of market globalists has shifted to widespread concerns that their attempt to surpass the nation-state has gone too far and must be stopped. Many commentators now reinforce the idea that the integration of markets and societies has not lived up to its promises. This rising "globophobia" is also a subject in popular culture within particular national contexts.

The Russo-Ukrainian War and the COVID-19 pandemic in 2020 further tested globalization's integrative growth and the political stability of individual countries worldwide. These events reveal a deeper crisis that threatens the fundamental principles of liberal democracy. This concerning pattern is particularly evident in the decreasing trust in traditional representative governments. Citizens increasingly see a gap between politicians' promises and their own experiences, as they expect their governments to protect them from external threats associated with multiculturalism and immigration. Amid this democratic crisis, an identity crisis is also forming, fueled by resistance to globalization. This often leads rural communities to turn to their nation, local groups, and religion [11].

Against this backdrop, authoritarian populists gained traction by attacking cosmopolitan elites and promising to restore national sovereignty. Their emotionally resonant appeals often proved more persuasive than the rational assurances of neoliberal globalists. The belief in globalization as a linear path toward progress has given way to a more fragmented and ambivalent outlook, where global integration is no longer seen as inevitable or necessarily desirable. In this context, the concept of globalization has shifted from a symbol of boundless opportunity to a focal point of resistance and critique. What began as a promise of global unity has increasingly come to represent dislocation, inequality, and cultural conflict. For the generation that has experienced this period, globalization was the foundation for ensuring the universal principles of freedom, rights, property, and mobility, as established in the American-led neoliberal world order. While for the generation living with the security and ecological threats of the future, globalization is a part of the lived political and social structures that pose existential challenges. This interpretative transformation reflects deeper changes in how societies understand power, identity, and belonging in an interconnected—but not necessarily unified—world.

3. Key contributions and limitations of global studies

The aforementioned perceptual shift requires compiling the main contributions that have impacted research by applying the lens of "global issues" within the social sciences and humanities while engaging with both contemporary and historical processes. In their book "Globalization Matters," Manfred B. Steger and Paul James highlight the innovativeness of global studies, which not only cover their techno-economic aspects but also explore their much-neglected sociocultural and political dimensions. The authors identify three main research contributions implementing global dimensions.

The first major contribution was Roland Robertson's effort to introduce "globalization" into the social sciences. In the early 1990s, he expanded the Marxist, economistic view of globalization—focused on marketization as a material process—and emphasized the cultural and subjective aspects often overlooked in popular discourse. His influential definition of globalization includes two key dimensions: the growing transnational social connections and the development of a reflexive global consciousness [12, 13]. Additionally, he promoted the term "glocalization," which further acknowledged the social dimension within the concept of globalization. Robertson argued that through social interactions, the global constantly intersects with the local, making globalization not just a distant process on a large scale but something that is truly tangible and observable at the local level [14].

The second major contribution was Arjun Appadurai's insights into the flows of material culture, which serve as resources for new identities and subjectivities that are no longer tied to the modern nation or the traditional tribe [15]. He suggested that the main forces behind global economic, cultural, and political changes can be understood through five types of global "landscapes": "ethnoscapes" (the movement of people), "mediascapes" (the spread of media and information), "technoscapes" (the flow of technology), "finanscapes" (the movement of money and capital), and "ideoscapes" (the spread of political ideas and values). These "landscapes" shape how individuals and societies imagine and make sense of today's highly interconnected world. Although people, ideas, and goods have always moved across regions throughout history, Appadurai pointed out that the speed, scale, and complexity of these global flows today are unprecedented. As a result, the mismatches or "disjunctures" between these flows have become a central issue in what he calls the "politics of global culture" [16]. These "disjunctures" in how goods, services, information, and ideas move around the world have led to the formation of many different kinds of "worlds." These worlds are shaped by the unique historical and political contexts of the people and groups involved, even if they are spread across different parts of the globe. Examples of such worlds include transnational corporations, nation-states, diaspora communities, nongovernmental organizations (NGOs), and local or regional movements and groups.

The third highlighted contribution is Saskia Sassen's idea of connecting globalization to major urban cities around the world. While these urban areas had already served as important international centers for business and culture, Sassen argued that recent globalization has brought about significant and simultaneous changes in their economies, urban layouts, and social structures. As a result, global cities have become especially vital as central hubs where global networks converge, including the movement of people, ideas, goods, and money. This is why, she claimed, global cities are worth studying as complex systems that manage and influence a wide range of activities crossing national borders [17].

The contributions within global studies have also impacted related disciplines like historical studies, where global history has gained increasing prominence in recent decades, offering new frameworks for understanding historical processes. However, this development has also been met with criticism, particularly from empirically grounded historians. As Sebastian Conrad points out, one of the main objections to global perspectives in historical studies concerns the reliance on secondary sources and synthesized literature [18]. Critics argue that global historians often operate at a macro-level, distancing themselves from the meticulous archival work and primary source analysis that lead to more nuanced and potentially groundbreaking outcomes. The argument is that the macro-level orientation comes with certain methodological limitations. Because the scale of analysis tends to be broad, the selection of sources often becomes narrow and standardized, drawing primarily on already interpreted material. This can lead to uniform narratives that lack the nuance and diversity of perspectives found in microhistorical or locally grounded studies. Furthermore, global approaches sometimes struggle to capture the complexity of specific historical contexts, particularly when local dynamics are flattened in favor of overarching structural explanations.

Despite these limitations, global history provides valuable contributions to the contextualization of historical phenomena. It encourages historians to situate local events within larger transnational and transregional contexts. This expanded contextualization demands more rigorous analytical methods, prompting scholars to explain how global forces influence local specifics. In this way, global history elevates the standards for historians' interpretive work by pushing them to consider broader spatial and temporal scales while remaining focused on detail.

At the same time, many global historical studies rely on broad overviews rather than detailed monographs. However, these syntheses play a vital role in the field: they help outline the overall shape of global processes and highlight patterns that might be overlooked from narrower perspectives. When combined with empirical case studies, global viewpoints can provide a complementary lens that expands our understanding of how historical developments are connected. The challenge lies in developing methods that bridge the gap between global frameworks and local evidence, ensuring that the richness of empirical detail is not lost in the pursuit of larger narratives.

4. On the role of multidisciplinarity and empirical exemplification in studying global issues

As the concept of globalization evolves, there is a need to develop better tools and perspectives for its analysis. While global history has broadened the scope of historical research, it also emphasizes a wider need in global studies: combining multidisciplinary methods and empirical evidence. Until very recently, historians have looked at the past with the tools of the nineteenth century. But globalization has fundamentally altered our ways of knowing, and it is no longer possible to study nations in isolation or to understand world history as emanating from the West. These are not just methodological choices—they are crucial strategies for deepening the quality and credibility of global inquiries. Global issues such as climate change, migration, economic inequality, or cultural conflict do not conform to any particular boundaries. They are inherently complex and dynamic, requiring insights from a range of disciplines, including history, sociology, political science, economics, and communication studies, among others. A multidisciplinary approach enables the consideration of complementary perspectives and has the potential to avoid overly deterministic or one-dimensional narratives that risk flattening the human experience.

The importance of empirical exemplification lies in the careful selection of cases, context-specific examples that illustrate how global processes operate in a local context. These empirical cases do more than merely "prove" theories; they help challenge and refine them. For instance, while global issues can influence new identity formations, detailed studies of particular communities impacted by liberalization can reveal underlying dynamics, such as cultural changes, resistance movements, or environmental issues. Such case studies ground global discourses in actual lived experiences, enhancing the accountability and relevance of the analysis.

Moreover, empirical exemplification serves an essential function in public and policy debates. Abstract discussions about "global capitalism" or "transnational governance" can remain inaccessible or disengaged from the concerns of everyday life. However, when these ideas are connected to concrete examples—such as community displacement or the rise of a transnational populist movement—they become more relevant and urgent. This opens up opportunities for more inclusive and democratic dialog across academic disciplines and political and civic spheres and stimulates the formulation of original yet challenging research questions that help extend disciplinary borders: How do we write a global history that is not Eurocentric but does not fall into the trap of creating new centers? What are the politics involved in global history? etc.

In the context of global history, combining a global perspective with detailed empirical work—whether through case studies, oral histories, or archival research—provides a means to mediate between the macro and the micro, the general and the specific. It acknowledges that while global structures shape local lives, local agency also reshapes global processes. This dialectical view enriches our understanding of globalization not as a top-down force, but as an ongoing negotiation between structures and people.

Author details

Izabela A. Dahl
School of Humanities, Education and Social Sciences, Örebro University, Sweden

*Address all correspondence to: izabela.dahl@oru.se

IntechOpen

© 2025 The Author(s). Licensee IntechOpen. This chapter is distributed under the terms of the Creative Commons Attribution License (http://creativecommons.org/licenses/by/4.0), which permits unrestricted use, distribution, and reproduction in any medium, provided the original work is properly cited.

References

[1] Annan K. The Politics of Globalization. Massachusetts. Available from: https://academy.wcfia.harvard.edu/politics-globalization-hon-kofi-annan: Cambridge; 1998 [Accessed: June 30, 2025]

[2] Nordin S. Globaliseringens Idéhistoria. Lund: Studentlitteratur; 2006. pp. 125-128

[3] Castell M. The Information Age: Economy, Society and Culture. Vol. 1-3. Oxford/Malden MA: Blackwell; 1996-1998

[4] Steger MB, James P. What is happening to globalization? In: Globalization Matters. Engaging the Global in Unsettled Times. Cambridge: Cambridge University Press; 2019. pp. 1-19

[5] Darian-Smith E, McCarty PC. The Global Turn. Berkeley: University of California Press; 2017

[6] Steger MB, Wahlrab A. What Is Global Studies? Theory & Practice. London & New York: Routledge; 2017

[7] King S. Grave New World: The End of Globalization and the Return of History. New Haven: Yale University Press; 2017

[8] Galston W. Anti-Pluralism: The Populist Threat to Liberal Democracy. New Haven: Yale University Press; 2018

[9] Judis J. The Nationalist Revival. Trade, Immigration, and the Revolt against Globalization. New York: Columbia Global Reports; 2018

[10] Norris P, Inglehart R. Cultural Backlash. Trump, Brexit, and Authoritarian Populism. Cambridge: Cambridge University Press; 2019

[11] Castells M. Rupture. The Crisis of Liberal Democracy. Cambridge: Polity Press; 2019

[12] Robertson R. Mapping the global condition: Globalization as the central concept. Theory, Culture and Society. 1990;**2-3**:15-30

[13] Robertson R. Globalization: Social Theory and Global Culture. London: Sage Publications; 1992

[14] Robertson R. Globalisation or glocalization? Journal of International Communication. 1994;**1**:33-52

[15] Appadurai A. Disjuncture and difference in the global cultural economy. Theory, Culture and Society. 1990;**2-3**:295-310

[16] Appadurai A. Modernity at Large: Cultural Dimensions of Globalization. Minneapolis: University of Minnesota Press; 1996

[17] Sassen S. The Global City: New York, London, Tokyo. Princeton: Princeton University Press; 2001

[18] Conrad S. What Is Global History? Princeton: Princeton University Press; 2017

Chapter 2

Conservative Revolution and Nationalism

Tihomir Cipek

Abstract

The text uses the theory of nationalism to analyze the fundamental ideas of the conservative revolution. This is done through the reconstruction of the basic theses of the political thought of Thomas Mann, Arthur Moeller van den Bruck, Ernst Jünger, Oswald Spengler and Carl Schmitt. The analysis is focused on the way in which they interpreted the relationship between language and nation, war and nation, liberalism and nation, and the nation's relationship with the West. It has shown that language was thought to reflect the spirit of the nation, that war was considered as the foundation of the national identity, that liberalism was given the role of the main ideological enemy of German national identity, and that the West was rejected while Russia and Dostoevsky were praised. The subsequent conclusion is that the ideology of the conservative revolution was based on German nationalism and the rejection of liberalism. Finally, it has been noted that, although conservative revolutionaries advocated for a dictatorship, they did not want a return to the old regime of the monarchy but an authoritarian conservative utopia. It is precisely those utopian elements of the conservative revolution that still make its ideas appealing to the radical right.

Keywords: conservative revolution, nationalism, war, liberalism, the west, conservative utopia

1. Introduction

The term conservative revolution entered academic discussion thanks to Armin Mohler's dissertation: *Die Konservativ Revolution in Deutschland 1918–1932*. This was a doctoral thesis defended in 1949 at the University of Basel, which contains about a hundred annotated biographies and bibliographies of political thinkers whom Mohler considered to be conservative revolutionaries.[1] Mohler's dissertation has since prompted two conflicting views. Some, like Volker Weiß [1], believe that it was a kind of rehabilitation of fascism, while others, like Hennig Ottman [2], hold it to be a legitimate academic work. Ottman further believes that, not only is the work scientifically correct, but that the theoreticians whom Mohler has included in the conservative revolution – though

---

[1] This ideological movement also counted as its members writers Arthur Moeller van den Bruck, Thomas Mann, Ernst Jürgen, Hans Grimm, philosopher Oswald Spengler, politician Edgar Julius Jung, jurist Carl Schmitt, and many others.

they undeniably share some fascist ideas – are not fascists but represent a separate phenomenon in the history of political ideas. It is interesting that Mohler's mentor, Karl Jaspers, was also aware of the controversial German-nationalist political charge in his doctoral thesis. That is why he felt the need to mention that he would not have been able to take responsibility for Mohler's dissertation if he had not known that Germany would politically become completely marginal, seeing how, after the Second World War, all political relations would be determined by the USA and the USSR ([1], p. 47). Clearly, Mohler's book has been causing controversy in academic circles from the very beginning. But the discussion about the conservative revolution only moved to the general public with the emergence of the ideology of the new right, gathered around Alain de Benoist.[2] The interest became even greater after radical, populist right-wing parties entered the parliaments of a number of European countries in the late twentieth and early 21st century. This has sparked a new debate on the conservative revolution [4].[3]

Namely, even the opponents of this term, such as the German sociologist Stefan Breuer, conceded that it was one of the "greatest creations in the recent history of political ideas" ([8], p. 5)[4]. This is due to the fact that the concept of conservative revolution was, among other things, well suited for describing and analyzing the ideology of contemporary right-wing populist parties. After all, today, it is obvious that, just as at the time of the original ideology of the conservative revolution, the political competition does not solely revolve around material interests but also around the way in which politics will define the role of identities [9]. And in that struggle, the way we define terms is of crucial importance. This is a conflict related to the determination of "true" values, which is why the analysis of political phenomena once again places importance on concepts such as Max Weber's "life conduct" or Georg Simmel's "style of life."

The conservative revolution thus represented a struggle to define a national identity that was reflected in culture, but that does not mean that it was not also a class struggle. Namely, in late (post-industrial) capitalism, class should not be defined just in economic terms, through material resources that a class possesses or that are denied to them, but also through its identity as related to its lifestyle and culture [10]. Moreover, the strength of the new right-wing movements in Europe clearly shows that the liberal thesis of Ulrich Beck [11] – according to which we are entering a classless age, in which an individual chooses their own destiny, is simply not true. I believe that it is precisely the ideas of the conservative revolution that reveal the limits of the liberal interpretation of lifeworld. That is why the thinkers of the conservative revolution concerned themselves with language, myth, religion and national identity. Of course, this does not mean that the definitions of ideological terms do not hide specific material interests.

However, this text will focus on the ideology, or rather the ideas of the conservative revolution with regard to the phenomenon of nationalism. Namely, it seems that we are witnessing the return of nationalism in Europe and the weakening of the European utopia. This is reflected in the rise of right-wing parties whose ideology is centred on the

---

[2] An overview of the new right's ideas is provided by Tomislav Sunić [3].

[3] In Croatian social sciences and humanities, this term is covered in the texts of Damir Velički [5] and Domagoj Tomas [6], in which the authors discuss the ideas of the new right. It is also mentioned in Rade Kalanj's article [7], which draws a connection between neoliberalism and conservatism. Although these are excellent texts, the conservative revolution is thematized only with regard to other phenomena.

[4] All quotes, except the ones from works by Oswald Spengler's *The Decline of the West*, Moeller van den Bruck, Ishay Landa, and Thomas Mann's *Reflections of a Nonpolitical Man* were translated by the author (into Croatian) and the translator of the paper (into English).

defense of the nation and the state [12]. Nationalism is still the most powerful principle of political legitimacy in the modern world, and the nation-state is – institutionally and historically speaking – the only true space of democracy ([13], p. 12). This text will therefore try to reconstruct the key ideas of the conservative revolution and examine their connection with the basic features of the nationalist ideology. Nationalism rests on three key demands: for an authentic national identity, which is reflected in the language and separates us from those others – in an extreme case, separates friends from enemies; for the reconstruction of the "real" history of a nation, its golden age; and finally, nationalism seeks the true "home" of a nation, that is, the real or imaginary space, the territory of the nation ([14], pp. 208–209; [15], pp. 27–36). By utilizing qualitative discourse analysis, this paper will show which concepts occupy a central position in the discursive field of nationalism, and what is their place in the ideology of the conservative revolution. It starts from the thesis that the key function of concepts in political theory is to serve in the political struggle, and that the thinkers of the conservative revolution used them for exactly this purpose. It will show the connection between the language and the "spirit" of the nation, the interpretation of war as the pinnacle of national history, and the idea of the incompatibility of liberalism with a nation's "true" values. It will also consider the conservative revolutionaries' perspective on the West and Russia. This text will advance the argument that the appeal of the ideas of the conservative revolution lies in its advocacy of key nationalist values.

2. Language and the nation

The term "conservative revolution" first appeared as the title of a book by the Russian philosopher and writer Yuri Samarin. In his "Conservative Revolution," published in 1875, he advocated for the spiritual renewal of the Russian nation based on anti-Enlightenment and anti-liberal values. The concept of a conservative revolution was also used by the author of the theory of integral nationalism, Charles Maurras, in his work "Enquête sur la monarchie" from 1900. This term was further mentioned by Thomas Mann in the article "Russische Anthologie" from 1921 ([2], p. 143). However, it should be noted that this term actually became popular with the German and European public thanks to Hugo von Hofmannsthal. Von Hofmannsthal coined it by considering the relationship between the language and the nation. In 1927, he gave the inaugural lecture at the University of Munich entitled "Das Schrifttum als geistiger Raum der Nation" (The Written Word as the Spiritual Space of the Nation). In that lecture, Von Hofmannsthal explained that he was actually talking about a spiritual process that was current at that time. "Synthesis, so slow and magnificent – if one wants to look at it from the outside – so spooky and challenging, if we are in it […] The process of which I speak is nothing other than a conservative revolution on a scale […] that has so far been unknown in European history. Its goal is the formation of a new German reality in which the entire German nation can participate" ([16], p. 31)[5].

---

[5] "[Ich spreche von einem Prozess, in dem wir mitten inne stehen,] einer Synthese, so langsam und grossartig - wenn man sie von aussen zu sehen vermöchte - als finster und prüfend, wenn mani in ihr steht. […] Der Prozess, von dem ich rede, ist nischts anderes als eine konservative Revolutin von einem Unfange, wie die europäische Geschichte ihn nicht kennt. Ihr Ziel ist Form, eine neue deutsche Wirklichkeit, an der die ganze Nation teilnehmen könne." [T. C.]

To wit, von Hofmannstahl used the term conservative revolution to denote the spiritual process of awakening the nation. He believed that spiritual renewal should enable the German people to counter the influences of the Renaissance, the Reformation and the French Enlightenment. He was motivated by the hope that the "new German reality," which he advocated, would enable a "new German unity." The task of this new national unity was to overcome the class and political divisions within the nation. Von Hofmannsthal believed that this process should only be indirectly political, because it actually represented a kind of a spiritual revolution. Von Hofmansthal derived his theses from the philosophy of Johann Gottfried Herder, who in turn believed that the spirit of the nation was reflected in the language ([17], p. 463; [18], pp. 83–84). That was why Von Hofmansthal strongly emphasized the inseparable connection between the language, the identity of a nation and national literature.[6] He claimed that the ties between the nation and the language, between the "nation and literature," could not be built on the idea of freedom but only through spiritual unity because he considered the spiritual unity of a nation to be higher than the freedom of the individual. That was why he wanted writers to become the true "priests" of a nation because he believed that "we find each other in the language, which is something very different than just a natural means of communication; for in it the past speaks to us, we are acted upon by forces that immediately become powerful, to which political institutions are not able to give space or set up obstacles, the unique connection between the sexes becomes effective, we feel that something is behind it and that something we dare to call the spirit of the nation" ([16], p. 9)[7]. This was a definition of language that was based on cultural essentialism, which emphasized the strict boundary between Us and Them. To this day, this has remained the central political function of linguistic purity: the separation from others and the unification of all members of a nation ([20], p. 51). Integral nationalism is, therefore, the hard core of the ideology of cultural revolution, but also of the ideology of the new right, which also believes that nations should be saved from the destructive effects of liberalism.

3. War and the nation

War is one of the key values of the conservative revolution. The idea that war restores and strengthens the nation appears in all the authors of the conservative revolution. The war is also one of the key legitimizing narratives of the new right. Here it should be noted that placing war at the centre of a national identity is actually not rare. War often functions as the founding myth of a nation, as is also the case with the Croatian nation [21]. For example, the German national founding myth is the 1871 war victory over France or an even earlier constructed myth about the victory of the Germanic peoples over the Romans in the Teutoburg Forest, led by Arminius (Hermann) in 9 AD. The founding myth of the nation in France is the French

---

[6] An example of this connection as relating to the Croatian nation was brought by Coha [19].

[7] "In einer Sprache finden wir uns zueinander, die völlig etwas anderes ist als das bloße natürliche Verständigungsmittel; denn in ihr redet Vergangenes zu uns, Kräfte wirken auf uns ein und werden unmittelbar gewaltig, denn die politischen Einrichtungen weder Raum zu geben, noch Schranken zu setzen mächtig sind, ein eigentümlicher Zusammenhang wird wirksam zwischen den Geschlechtern, wir ahnen dahinter ein Etwas waltend, das wir den Geist der Nation zu nennen uns getrauen." [T. C.].

Revolution of 1789, while the same role in the United States is played by the American War of Independence (1775–1783). For the German ideologues of the conservative revolution, the central myth is the Great War.[8]

Even the experience of defeat did not prevent German conservative revolutionaries from celebrating war. By celebrating war, they celebrated the struggle of men, war heroism and sacrifices for the national community. It did not matter if they themselves had experienced war. In fact, this was rare in their ranks. The exception was Ernst Jünger, a true warrior with extensive combat experience. Unlike him, the founder of the conservative revolution movement, Moeller van den Bruck, was not directly involved in armed struggle but served as a propaganda officer on the Eastern Front. Other conservative revolutionaries, such as Thomas Mann, Oswald Spengler, Werner Sombart and Max Scheler, made their contribution to the war at the writing desk. But this did not prevent them from claiming that war had some higher meaning, a deep and powerful existential significance for the entire German nation. They turned war into a medium for shaping a better, stronger man and a new energetic nation. It could actually be said that they turned war into a kind of political religion.

Believing in war was becoming more important than Christianity. Moreover, unlike the old conservatives, the conservative revolutionaries did not, as a rule, rely on classic religion; their political programme was their faith. However, this does not mean that they were not interested in spirituality. On the contrary, one of their central goals was the restoration of the nation's true spiritual life, and they insisted that it was possible only if war was placed at the centre of the nation's spiritual experience. This was the birth of a radical right-wing political religion, which believed that the restoration of the German nation was possible only if it returned to wartime heroism and broke with the dull routine of Weimar Republic's decadent civil life. Conservative revolutionaries thus believed that this "new conservative order" could only be established by a true revolution of the national spirit ([23], p. 11).

These advocates of revolution also did not shy away from physical violence. Violence was not understood as something that would happen spontaneously, as an outburst of rage and bitterness that turns into violence, but as a carefully planned action. This plan hinged on choosing the right time, recognizing the right moment when violence should be used. The task of ideology was to search for that revolutionary moment. The central place that violence occupied in this type of conservative ideology was well illustrated by Ernst Jünger's 1926 exclamation. "Revolution, revolution! This is what must be preached constantly, defiantly, systematically, relentlessly" ([24], p. 215). His pathetic call for a revolution was closely related to the experience of war. Namely, in his political thought, war was reduced solely to a heroic experience and represented a key sign of masculinity. In his work "War as an Inner Experience" Jünger composed a "passionate hymn to war," as noted by Karl Mueller Frøland ([25], p. 141). Jünger described warriors in an extremely romantic way, as people filled with passion, instinct and a beastly drive, people who put themselves in the service of the nation. "The war created a new dangerous crowd of people, let's put this crowd into action!" said Jünger [24]. Oswald Spengler, another conservative revolutionary, believed that war was an inevitable, essential feature of relations between nations. "A people *is*, really, only in relation to peoples. But the natural, 'race,' relation between them is for that very reason a relation of war — this is a fact that no truths avail to

---

[8] A similar use of the Homeland War can also be found in Croatian politics [22].

alter. War is the primary politics of *everything* that lives, and so much so that in the deeps battle and life are one, and being and will-to-battle expire together" ([26], p. 440).

It should therefore be concluded that the ideologues of the conservative revolution considered war to be the pinnacle of national history. War was understood as a phenomenon that enabled a nation to be established in its entirety and to find the meaning of its existence. They believed that it was the experience of the Great War that allowed the penetration of the German national spirit into the life of every single member of the German nation. Besides the meaning they attached to war, another precondition for a nation's spiritual renewal and the establishment of an authoritarian political order that was preached by conservative revolutionaries was a decisive confrontation with liberalism.

4. Liberalism and the nation

The ideologues of the conservative revolution believed that the restoration of the nation could only follow after its main enemy, liberalism, was defeated.[9] They believed that liberalism broke the solid, organic unity of the national community and thus undermined the foundations of state power. These thinkers also considered their political opponents from the left to be mere products of liberalism. Conservative revolutionaries' disdain for liberalism was well summed up by the subtitle of a chapter in Arthur Moeller van den Bruck's book *Das dritte Reich* [28], which reads "Liberalism is the Death of Nations" ([29], p. 77). Pathetically, but completely assured, he claimed that liberalism: "[…] has undermined civilization, has destroyed religions, has ruined nations" ([29], p. 91). He concluded that liberalism was nothing more than "the self-dissolution of mankind" ([28], p. 80)[10].

Conservative revolutionaries, therefore, associated liberalism with a spiritual principle that stemmed from the Enlightenment and the 1789 French Revolution. This was a historical event that they truly despised and consequently rejected all its achievements: parliamentarism, the tripartite separation of powers, the rights of men and citizens; in short, all the values of liberal democracy. What bothered them the most about liberal ideology was individualism, because they believed that it was precisely individualism, with its doctrine of emphasizing the rights of the individual, that inevitably destroyed the unity of nations. In their opinion, the true national German political order could not be based on free individuals and the social contract. On the contrary, they emphasized that an individual could only effect the meaning of their existence in a national community. Community thus represented a primary value. That was why Spengler emphasized that: "Not 'I' but 'we'—a feeling of community to which every individual sacrifices his whole being. The individual does not matter; he must offer himself to the totality" ([30], pp. 31–32)[11]. So, an individual could only realize the meaning of their existence as a member of a community or, even more clearly, "only in the service to the community" ([31], p. 138). The central ideal of the

---

[9] The opposite interpretation, which tried to show that there was a connection between economic liberalism, fascism and neoliberalism, was made by Tomaž Mastnak [27].

[10] "*Selbstauflösung der Menschheit*". This sentence is missing from the authorized English edition (1934); translated from German original (1923) [T. C.].

[11] "*Kein 'Ich', sonder ein 'Wir', ein Gemeingefühl, in dem jeder mit seinem gesamten Dasein aufgeht.*" [T. C.]

conservative revolution was a national community, in which the interactions between people were based on emotional ties, rather than a society in which relations between people were based on interests. This ideal directed them towards rejecting even the idea of human rights. They, in fact, claimed that there could be no genuine individual rights that an individual could possess before entering into life with other people. Moreover, Spengler insisted that: "'Equal rights' are contrary to nature, are an indication of the departure from type of ageing societies, are the beginning of their irrevocable decline" ([32], p. 92). Liberalism was decisively rejected precisely because it was "an expression of society, which was no longer a community" ([28], p. 78)[12]. The national community could only be established through struggle, or more precisely through a conservative revolution. Conservative revolutionaries did not want compromise or a reconciliation of opposing forces, but struggle. Spengler also rejected the Enlightenment and liberal idea of the Western culture, based on science and technology, as the best for all mankind. On the contrary, he believed that all cultures were equal and that they grew naturally from their environment like plants. They lived and grew by themselves until they were ruined by the Western civilization, which reached its highest expression in big cities ([33], p. 181). He concluded that civilization robed cultures of their soul because it was "dying from atheism and nihilism" ([2], p. 171).

One of the most prominent theorists of conservative revolution, Carl Schmitt, resolutely attacked the liberal affinity for compromise.[13] He argued that, in its search for a compromise that was actually an effort to establish some kind of pure moral or pure economic state, liberalism showed that it actually did not understand the political, because it was deceived by the dynamics of discussion and the principle of competition ([35], p. 58). And because it ignored the political, Schmitt claimed, liberalism also ignored the state [36]. Namely, it was the state that decided on the political, because it made decisions about war and peace ([35], pp. 33–34). Another interpretation could be that it was Schmitt who abolished the link between politics and the state, and with his concept of the political tied politics to society ([37], p. 760). I would, however, support the exact opposite thesis, i.e. that Schmitt's concept of the political was strongly linked to the state ([38], p. 32; [39], p. 187; [40], p. 195; [41], p. 274). Whatever interpretation we accept, Carl Schmitt undoubtedly believed that it was the political that made a people into *a people*, and that, by abandoning the political, liberalism was actually destroying the people.[14] In a scathing tone, Schmitt decisively claimed that: "If a people no longer possessest the energy or the will to maintain itself in the sphere of politics, the latter will not thereby vanish from the world. Only a weak people will disappear" ([42], p.53). The political, according to

---

[12] *"Der Liberalismus ist der Ausdruck einer Gesellschaft, die nicht mehr Gemeinschaft ist"*. This sentence is missing from the authorized English edition (1934); translated from the German original (1923) [T. C.].

[13] An interesting interpretation that establishes a connection between liberalism and Carl Schmitt's theory is provided by Ishay Landa who claims that "Schmitt was thus anti-liberal indeed, but in a very liberal way. He embraced dictatorship to avert the triumph and rescind the gains, political and hence economical, of popular democracy." ([34], p. 186–187).

[14] A great comment on Schmitt's strong opposition to the year 1789 and its consequences is provided by Žarko Paić, who claims that, for Schmitt, "no counter-revolution is counter-revolutionary enough". And further: "Just as revolutionaries want to change the world, counter-revolutionaries want to neutralize and suspend the effect of every counter-revolution" ([40], p. 264). But at the same time, he notes that freedom has been neutralized precisely through modern depoliticization, which "wears the mask of liberalism" ([40], p. 263).

Schmitt, was superior to liberal values, to discussion and competition. He further claimed that a nation must necessarily be able to exist in a friend-enemy relationship[15] and, moreover, that this relationship was mediated by the state, because it was the state that, due to its exclusive right of making decisions on war and peace, essentially determined a nation's history. By ignoring the political, Schmitt concluded, liberalism ignored the state and, thereby the nation.

5. The west and the nation

Although the public today often thinks that the ideas of the conservative revolution praised the West and chastised the East, the facts are exactly the opposite. Namely, the ideologues of the conservative revolution had great reservations about the West because the West tried to impose liberalism on all nations. Contrary to liberal universalism, the ideology of the conservative revolution was based on the thesis that each nation must find its own form of the state, i.e. political rule. Hence, they believed that liberal democracy must not become a universal order. The ideologues of the conservative revolution were particularly critical of England because they spread the idea of parliamentarism. France, on the other hand, was despised because of the Enlightenment and the ideas of the 1789 revolution. In short, the West was considered to be the source of individualism and selfish egoism that destroyed solidarity within nations. Furthermore, these thinkers were also very critical of the Western glorification of technology because they believed that it disrupted the direct connection between man and nature, which they thought represented a strong foundation for and a virtue of the German national spirit. Moreover, they claimed that the dominance of technology and liberalism threatened the special path of the German nation, which should have led it to rise to world-historical power. Therefore, they countered the idea of the West with that of a German Central Europe, which was supposed to protect the Germans from the liberalism of France and Russia's tsarist autocracy. It was therefore necessary to show that the Germans were neither the West nor the East and that they could build a special authoritarian order.

This new order, which was supposed to reflect the spirit of the German nation, was called "Das dritte Reich" by Moeller van den Bruck in the title of his 1923 book. Here it should be noted that his concept of the Third Reich was fundamentally different from the Nazi one. Moeller van den Bruck, namely, did not advocate for racist laws, genocide against Jews or concentration camps. But there is no doubt that he was an opponent of liberal democracy and that his ideal was an authoritarian dictatorship. This order was supposed to be established through a conservative revolution. Van den Bruck believed that conservatism and revolution were not mutually exclusive but complemented each other. He asserted that "conservatism seizes directly on the revolution, through it and beyond it saves the life" which is "nevertheless the only life possible." "It is founded on the laws of nature, and Nature is always conservative" ([29], p. 193).

We have seen that conservatism was understood as a natural principle. This begs the question, where could one find this principle at work? Where was that

---

[15] It could also be argued that, in Schmitt, the political was reduced to the intensity of the relationship with the enemy, and that the content of the political was actually lost because "everyone can be a potential enemy" ([39], p. 185).

original man who was connected with nature? Where were the original conservative values preserved? Supporters of the conservative revolution found the answers to those questions in Russia. That country became a kind of a role model for them, and Dostoevsky became their favorite writer. Oswald Spengler claimed that Russia was the harbinger of a new culture. According to him, the Russian spirit was still not enslaved by destructive technology, and could thus allow human life in harmony with nature.[16] The original Russian spirit was "opposed to the Enlightenment," "the materialism of world-cities," which led to "cities of alien type" fixing themselves "like ulcers [...] in the townless land with its primitive peasantry" ([26], p. 193). Like most German conservatives, he despised Peter the Great, the emperor who had opened Russia to the West. Spengler claimed that Peter the Great became the evil scourge of Russia (*Russentums*) and concluded that "The primitive tsarism of Moscow is the only form which is even today appropriate to the Russian world, but in Petersburg it was distorted to the dynastic form of western Europe" ([26], p. 181). But, despite those difficulties, he still believed that Russia had a future because it could break away from the West (he also considered the Bolsheviks to be a product of the West).[17] Spengler felt that Dostoevsky was "the coming Russia," while "the inner Tolstoi" was "tied to the West" ([26], p. 194), and believed that the West would inevitably fail in Russia simply because it was opposed to the original spirit of the Russian nation.

Like Spengler, Thomas Mann favored Russia and Dostoevsky, and was skeptical of the West ([43], pp. 37–39). Mann quoted Dostoevsky's question that reflected his fear for the future of Germany: "Could it really be true that cosmopolitan radicalism has already taken roots in Germany, too?" ([44], p. 47). His answer makes it obvious that he shared Dostoevsky's hope that cosmopolitanism in Germany would not succeed, and that there was still such a thing as an original German spirit, some true patriotism that had been shaped by the ideas of Schopenhauer, Nietzsche and Wagner ([43], p. 69). Moreover, he considered Nietzsche to be the spiritual father of the conservative revolution because Nietzsche's thought combined "enlightenment and faith, freedom and slavery, spirit and flesh, 'God' and 'the world.' It is, expressed artistically, a combination of sentimentality and criticism, politically expressed, a combination of conservatism and revolution. [...] Nietzsche himself from the beginning [...] was nothing but a conservative revolution" ([45], p. 598).

It is worth noting that Thomas Mann identified democracy with politics. For him, politics could never have been anything but democratic. "One is a politician or one is not. And if one is, then one is democratic. The political-intellectual attitude is the democratic one; belief in politics is belief in democracy, in the *contrat social*" ([44], str. 16). It is thus quite clear why Mann called his work, which was crucial for understanding his relationship to the ideas of the conservative revolution, "Reflections of a Nonpolitical Man." Mann simply lamented the fact that democracy was progressing, as he believed that the democratic political order had "little or nothing to do with the higher intellectual life of the nation" ([44], p. 180). He believed that democracy was to blame for a state being formed in Germany that was "not particularly worthy of admiration. As egalitarian and as tolerant as it is, it no longer represents a definite world view

---

[16] This praise stemmed from Spengler's understanding of culture and civilization. Culture was what grew naturally, something that was not polluted by civilization.

[17] "For the Bolshevists are not the nation, or even a part of it, but the lowest stratum of this Petrine society, alien and western like the other strata [...] It is all megalopolitan and 'civilized'" ([26], p. 196).

[...]. A hundred forces are working on the disintegration of national culture and on the internationalization of life" ([44], p. 180). Mann thought that the despicable internationalism was coming from England and France, the central states of the West. It could therefore be concluded that Thomas Mann saw the West as an enemy of the original German national spirit. After all, other conservative revolutionaries also believed that the West was their main enemy because of its Enlightenment and liberalism.[18]

Of course, there is no doubt that conservative and revolutionary principles, in their ideal-type form, are opposed to each other. Supporters of the conservative revolution resolved this contradiction in favor of conservatism. So, although they advocated for a coup, they believed that conservatism was in agreement with the laws of the people's life, and was thus superior to a revolution. Accordingly, they claimed that, despite inter-party conflicts, German national unity that had been achieved in the war would turn into the "*esprit des corps*"[19] of the German nation, into a feeling of "fate-fraught sense of cohesion" ([29], p. 36). The idea of restoring the unity of the nation was, therefore, the central idea of the conservative revolution. The prevailing conclusion was that the nation would be rebuilt only when political liberalism had been destroyed. Only very few of them, like Ernst Niekisch [46], wanted to destroy not just political liberalism, but also the economic form of liberalism, capitalism. Some, like Thomas Mann, criticized the "dominance of money" that marked the epoch of "materialism" ([44], p. 262). However, despite this criticism, conservative revolutionaries – just like the Nazis and the fascists – did not question capitalism as such, but were content with attacking liberal ideas of individual freedom and rights, as well as liberal democracy and the republic [47]. Most thinkers of the conservative revolution believed that capitalism could somehow be forced to serve the nation. So, in principle, just as with the entire so-called German anti-modernist perspective, there was a willingness to accept "some results of the civic civilization (such as capitalism, imperialist politics, industrial production, technology)" ([48], p. 118). It should be emphasized again that conservative revolutionaries believed that a compromise could be made with some material forms of the modern era, but that they resolutely rejected its political form: liberal democracy. They saw this confrontation with the modern liberal-democratic political order as their main mission. They countered the bitter reality of the Weimar Republic with their conservative-revolutionary utopia. It was a utopia that was supposed to enable the creation of a new sovereign state and a new "national community."

6. Conclusion

The aim of this paper was to interpret the ideology of the conservative revolution in a new way, by using the theory of nationalism, or rather the ideal-type examples of

---

[18] It seems that today's new right has the same enemies. As a rule, it does not consider Islam to be a threat in itself, but it emphasizes the importance of keeping it exclusively in the countries where it originally arose. Moreover, the New Right even sees Islam as a welcome potential ally in the fight against their main enemy, liberalism. The same applies to their animosities towards the city. The new right has retained the skepticism that the ideologues of the conservative revolution had towards the city. The openness of the city to the new, to the settlers, is unacceptable to them, because it necessarily leads to the mixing of cultures. Openness towards technology, modernization, new ideas on gender rights – the new right finds all of this is suspicious and unacceptable [1].

[19] "Esprit des corps" stands for the "*verinnerlichtes Daßein*" in German original ([28]., p. 20) [T. C.].

that thought. Of course, this does not mean that the interpretations of the conservative revolution that start from the crisis of the Enlightenment and modernity are not correct. But they have become commonplace, and can only partly explain why the radical and extreme right always goes back to the ideas of the conservative revolution. The real reason for this returning lies in integral nationalism, which forms the core of the ideology of the conservative revolution as well as the new radical right. They are connected by this type of nationalism, which has been shown to always gain strong political energy in times of crisis. That is why we are now witnessing the rise of radical right-wing parties. The paper has demonstrated that the ideology of the conservative revolution contained all the basic motifs of nationalism. First, the demand for the formation of a clear national identity, emphasizing the difference between "us" and "them." In this discourse, the values of our nation supersede all other values, and the ethnically defined nation is the only source of political legitimacy. This special identity of the nation is constructed by insisting on the idea that the spirit of the nation lies in its language. The second, a typical nationalist interpretation present among conservative revolutionaries, was the thesis that a nation has a special historical time, in which it reaches its height and achieves national unity. Conservative revolutionaries believed that this was achieved through war. That is why they glorified the First World War and reduced politics to a struggle between the nation and those others. They also claimed that nations experienced times of danger. One such time was the era of the 1789 French Revolution, which polluted the spirit of the German nation with the ideas of the Enlightenment, liberalism and leftist thought. In general, the conservative revolutionaries obsessively emphasized the importance of national history, which was always interpreted in such a way as to glorify one's own nation and deny the crimes committed in its name. The third nationalist motif was the demand for a special space of the nation. This space, according to the interpretation of conservative revolutionaries, should be separate from the West, should include all members of the ethnically defined nation, and should provide it with "living space," so that the nation can grow to its full historical strength. In addition to these three, typically nationalist demands – for a special identity, historical time and national territory ([14], pp. 208–209) – conservative revolutionaries presented a fourth demand, also based on nationalism. Namely, they believed that the German nation had to establish a special political order, which would defend it from liberal individualism that was destroying its unity. This order was given different names; Spengler spoke of "Prussian socialism"; but regardless of the term used to describe it, all of them advocated for some form of authoritarian dictatorship. It was a dictatorship that did not aim to end capitalism, but that was supposed to force it to serve the nation. Conservative revolutionaries, therefore, were not interested in preservation, in returning to the old, but wanted change and to fight for a new form of the conservative idea. Their ideology was centred on the question of creating a new authoritarian political order and emphasizing the need for the country's territory to overlap with the territory of the ethnically defined German nation. There is no doubt that this was an integral German nationalism, which sought the revival of the German nation.

This revival was not supposed to happen through a reactionary return to the glorious past, but a revolutionary journey into the new national future. This could have been achieved – according to the conservative revolutionaries – if literature and its language were established as the essence of the spirit of the nation, if the memory of war was instituted as an eternal national value, if liberalism, which with its advocacy of individualism was tearing apart the unity of the nation, was rejected and if the nation moved away from the West and returned to its authentic values. Although conservative revolutionaries repeated the typical myths of the nationalist ideology, they did not actually search for what determined the nation's past; by interpreting the past, they were trying to construct that which should be eternal for the nation in the future.

Some of these questions that the conservative revolutionaries posed to liberalism are still relevant today. Namely, it seems to me that liberal theses about globalism and the free individual have written the nation off too early. And that the current strengthening of right-wing nationalist parties is some sort of a revenge on the part of nationalism. So, on one hand, we are faced with a right-wing nationalist populism that cares exclusively for its own nation and is closed to others, and on the other, with a new liberalism, which insists on a society of unique and singular individuals who should only care about themselves. And a society in which an individual will confine themselves "entirely within the solitude of his own heart" ([49], p. 177) is not conducive to democratic participation.

It can be concluded that the ideas of the conservative revolution were based on basic nationalist demands for the creation of a homogeneous nation: that they were not reactionary because they were not advocating a return to the past but a revolutionary creation of a new, spiritually renewed nation that could develop its full strength within a new authoritarian social and political order, which had no place for liberal values. So, the utopian element of the conservative revolution seems undeniable, just as it is undeniable that a political order in which liberal values were not respected would be authoritarian. Given today's political circumstances, the ideas of the conservative revolution will continue to be attractive to the radical right. The rest are left to face, on one hand, radical liberalism, in which the individual is everything and the people are nothing, and on the other radical nationalism, in which the nation is everything and the individual is nothing. After all, there is no doubt that the conflict between cosmopolitanism and nationalism is an essential determinant of our times.

Author note

The article was published in the Croatian language in the *Politička misao* journal, 59 (1), 7–23.

Author details

Tihomir Cipek
Faculty of Political Science, University of Zagreb, Zagreb, Croatia

*Address all correspondence to: tcipek@fpzg.hr

IntechOpen

© 2024 The Author(s). Licensee IntechOpen. This chapter is distributed under the terms of the Creative Commons Attribution License (http://creativecommons.org/licenses/by/4.0), which permits unrestricted use, distribution, and reproduction in any medium, provided the original work is properly cited.

References

[1] Weiß V. Die autoritäre Revolte. Die "Neue Rechte" und der Untergang des Abendlandes. Stuttgart: Klett-Cotta; 2017

[2] Ottmann H. Geschichte des politischen Denkens. Von den Anfängen bei den Griechen bis auf unsere Zeit. Das 20. Jahrhundert. Der Totalitarismus und seine Überwindung. Stuttgart/Weimar, Band IV/1. Metzler. 2010

[3] Sunić T. Europska nova desnica. Korijeni, ideje i mislioci. Zagreb: Hasanbegović; 2009

[4] Fücks R, Becker C, editors. Das alte Denken der Neuen Rechten: Die langen Linien der antiliberalen Revolte. Frankfurt am Main: Wochenschau Verlag; 2020

[5] Velički D. Desni ekstremizam, radikalizam i zapadnoeuropska Nova desnica. Politička Misao. 2010;**47**(2):67-84

[6] Tomas D. Europska 'nova desnica' – marginalna politička misao ili ostvariv potencijal? Pilar: Časopis za Društvene i Humanističke Studije. 2013;**8**(15-16):113-131

[7] Kalanj R. Mijene i konjunkture konzervativizma. Revija za sociologiju. 1998;**29**:3-4

[8] Breuer S. Anatomie der Konservativen Revolution. Darmstadt: Wissenschaftliche Buchgesellschaft; 1993

[9] Fukuyama F. Identitet. Zahtjev za dostojanstvom i politike zamjeranja. Zagreb: TIM press; 2019

[10] Reckwitz A. Das Ende der Illusionen. Politik, Ökonomie und Kultur in der Spätmoderne. Berlin: Suhrkamp; 2019

[11] Beck U. Jenseits von Stand und Klasse? In: Kreckel R, editor. Soziale Ungleichheiten. (Soziale Welt. Sonderband 2). Göttingen: Schwartz; 1983

[12] Taguieff P-A. Antisemitizam. Zagreb: Tim Press; 2017. (L' antisémitisme, Croatian edition)

[13] Dahrendorf R. Die Krisen der Demokratie. Ein Gespräch mit Antonio Polito. München: C.H. Beck; 2002

[14] Özkirmli U. Theories of Nationalism. A Critical Introduction. London: Palgrave Macmillan; 2010

[15] Smith AD. Nationalism. Theory, Ideology, History. Cambridge, UK and Malden, MA, USA: Polity Press; 2010

[16] Von Hofmannsthal H. Das Schrifttum als geistiger Raum der Nation. München: Verlag der Bremmer Presse; 1927. Available from: https://ds.ub.uni-bielefeld.de/viewer/image/97830/2/#topDocAnchor

[17] Švoger V. Recepcija Herdera u hrvatskome narodnom preporodu. Časopis za Suvremenu Povijest. 1998;**30**(3):455-478

[18] Mance I. Zèrcalo naroda. Ivan Kukuljević Sakcinski: Povijest umjetnosti i politika. Zagreb: IPU; 2012

[19] Coha S. Medij, kultura, nacija. Poetika i politika Gajeve Danice, Hrvatska sveučilišna naklada. Zagreb: Filozofski fakultet; 2015

[20] Hobsbawm EJ. Nations and Nationalism since 1780. Programme, Myth, Reality. 3rd ed. Cambridge: Cambridge University Press; 1990

[21] Cipek T. Funkcija političkog mita. O koristi mitskog za demokraciju. Anali Hrvatskog Politološkog Društva. 2013;**9**(1):7-19

[22] Jović D. Rat i mit. Politika identiteta u suvremenoj Hrvatskoj. Zaprešić: Fraktura; 2017

[23] Mohler A. Die Konservative Revolution in Deutschland 1918-1932. Ein Handbuch. Dritte, um einen Ergänzungsband erweiterte Auflage. Darmstadt: Wissenschaftliche Buchgesellschaft; 1989

[24] Jünger E. Die nationalistische Revolution [1926]. In: Berggötz SO, editor. Politische Publizistik 1919-1933. Stuttgart: Klett-Cotta; 2001. pp. 213-216

[25] Müller Frøland C. Understanding Nazi Ideology: The Genesis and Impact of a Political Faith. Jefferson, New Carolina: McFarland; 2020

[26] Spengler O. The Decline of the West. Perspectives of World History, Vol. II, Transl. London: Charles Francis Atkinson, George Allen and Unwin LTD; 1928. Available from: https://archive.org/details/in.ernet.dli.2015.283129/page/n1/mode/2up

[27] Mastnak T. Liberalizem, fašizem, neoliberalizem. Ljubljana: Založba/*cf; 2015

[28] Moeller van den Bruck A. Das dritte Reich. Berlin: Ring Verlag; 1923

[29] Moeller van den Bruck A. Germany's Third Empire. Authorized English Edition (Condensed) by E. O. Lorimer. London: George Allen and Unwin Ltd.; 1934. Available from: https://archive.org/details/moeller-van-den-bruck-germanys-third-empire/page/n1/mode/2up

[30] Spengler O. Preußentum und Sozialismus. München: Verlag C. H. Beck; 1920

[31] Jung EJ. Die Herrschaft der Minderwertigen, ihr Zerfall und ihre Ablösung durch ein neues Reich. Berlin: Verlag der Deutschen Rundschau; 1930

[32] Spengler O. The Hour of Decision. Part One: Germany and World-Historical Evolution, Transl. London: Charles Francis Atkinson, George Allen and Unwin LTD.; 1934. Available from: https://archive.org/details/in.ernet.dli.2015.121879/page/n3/mode/2up

[33] Spengler O. Propast Zapada. Zagreb: Demetra; 2000. (Decline of West, Croatian edition)

[34] Landa I. The Apprentice's sorcerer, Liberal tradition and fascism. In: Studies in Critical Social Sciences. Vol. 18. Brill; 2010

[35] Schmitt C. Der Begriff des Politischen. München: Duncker and Humblot; 1932

[36] Cvijanović H. The limits of the political: Transcendent passions and Carl Schmitt's failure in providing a theory of political stability. Politička Misao. 2012;**49**(5):138-156

[37] Sunajko G. Ontologija objektivnog neprijatelja kao nebića: Hannah Arendt i Carl Schmitt. Filozofska Istraživanja. 2016;**36**(4):753-774

[38] Vollrath E. Kako je Carl Schmitt došao do svog pojma političkog? Politička Misao. 1989;**26**(1):30-47

[39] Demirović A. Das Scheitern der Agonistik. Zur kritischen Theorie des Politischen. In: Bohemann U, Sörensen P, editors. Kritische Theorie der Politik. Berlin: Suhrkamp; 2019

[40] Paić Ž. Doba oligarhije. Od informacijske ekonomije do politike događaja. Zagreb: Litteris; 2017

[41] Cipek T. The political versus the state? The relevance of Carl Schmitt's concept of the political. Teorija in Praksa. 2021;**58**(2):268-283

[42] Schmitt C. The Concept of the Political. Transl. George Schwab. Chicago: The University of Chicago Press; 2007

[43] Mann T. Razmatranja nepolitičnog čovjeka, prev. Zagreb, Disput: D. Lalović; 2018

[44] Mann T. Reflections of a Nonpolitical Man, Trans. Walter D. Morris. New York: Ungar; 1987

[45] Mann T. Gesammelte Werke in dreizehn Bänden. Russische Anthologie. Band 10. Frankfurt: Fischer; 1974. pp. 590-603

[46] Niekitsch E. Der Weg der deutschen Arbeiterschaft zum Staat. Berlin: Verlag der Neuen Gesellschaft; 1925

[47] Woods R. The Conservative Revolution in the Weimar Republic. New York, St: Martin's Press; 1996

[48] Kravar Z. Antimodernizam. AGM: Zagreb; 2003

[49] de Tocqueville A. O demokraciji u Americi. Zagreb: Fakultet političkih znanosti i Informator; 1995

Chapter 3

Globalization: Challenges and Effects on Europe Post-WWII

Izabela A. Dahl

Abstract

Globalization is often used in research as an empirical lens to examine ongoing developments over time, a process that integrates people and nations into larger structures and communities while dissolving traditional barriers. Historians argue that innovations in technology, transportation, and communication have driven globalization over the long term. However, a significant shift occurred with the end of the Cold War, which notably accelerated European political and economic integration. This study examines Europe's integration processes from a historical perspective and explores the differing development trajectories in Western and Eastern Europe before the collapse of the Soviet Union in terms of their political and economic progress toward the neoliberal democratic framework of the twentieth century. The central hypothesis of this contribution is that the divergent development paths of Eastern and Western Europe are primarily attributable to the Soviet Union's influence on international relations during the Cold War. However, some common development paths that extend beyond the political and ideological division of Europe can be recognized with respect to the shared need for welfare. This chapter explores the causes, challenges, and effects of European globalization, focusing on the key economic, political, and social factors that have influenced this process.

Keywords: globalization, European integration, cold war, East-West relations, development trajectories

1. Introduction

Globalization, as a transformative force, has reshaped the world and influenced the historical development of Europe, particularly in the post-World War II era. The devastation Europe faced in 1945—millions of lives lost, cities in ruins, and economies shattered—set the stage for an era of rebuilding that hinged on stabilizing society, restoring economic balance through international cooperation, and forming political alliances. This cooperation was pivotal in recovery and was particularly evident in the division of Europe, with Eastern European nations falling into the Soviet sphere of influence. Several countries, including Poland, Czechoslovakia, Hungary, the Baltic States, Bulgaria, and Romania, were absorbed into the Soviet Union's sphere of influence, marking a significant geopolitical shift that exacerbated the East-West divide defining much of the Cold War period.

The post-war era was a critical catalyst for modern European globalization regarding integration into global networks. While European globalization as a concept has roots that stretch back in time, long before the colonial past [1], the term is used chiefly empirically. Thus, it can describe the developments after World War II, particularly the economic, cultural, and political integration that accelerated the process. Moreover, notions of nationalism and geopolitics are interesting concepts in shaping 'individual and collective" causes and challenges to European globalization [2]. Additionally, the long-term drivers of the globalization process, such as technology, communication, and transportation, contributed to rapid changes and played a critical role in accelerating the process [3]. However, the divide between East and West resulted in vastly different political and economic development rates. It is essential to recognize this divergence when analyzing the broader process of globalization, as Western Europe moved swiftly toward a neoliberal democratic framework. Meanwhile, Eastern Europe remained constrained by communist economic practices until the early 1990s.

This chapter examines the integration processes in Europe prior to the collapse of the Soviet Union. It explores the interplay of political, economic, and social factors that shaped the Cold War era, emphasizing both conflict and cooperation toward the neoliberal democratic framework that characterized much of the twentieth century. In this regard, the analysis contributes to the history of globalization from a European perspective, focusing on how relations and exchanges evolved, including the development of common interests and values that transcended political and ideological divisions.

Using comparative and transfer-historical models, historians have long sought to move beyond the nationalistic scopes of interpretation in historical writing, especially when examining the far-reaching impacts of global processes. Although these approaches have been employed for some time, it was the end of the Cold War that accelerated interest in understanding globalization in a broader context, particularly due to the opening of many archives, which ensured more comprehensive accessibility of sources that provide crucial insights into developments extending beyond the East-West division of Europe. The diversity of sources enhances historical analysis as the evolution of Europe toward globalization unfolded over decades, with increasing economic integration and political cooperation serving as the foundation for contemporary global Europe. In this sense, the collapse of the Soviet Union in 1989 was a pivotal event that not only catalyzed the establishment of a single market and laid the groundwork for Europe's global prominence today [4] but also provided a better-informed analysis of the Cold War period in Europe.

The historical perspective on cross-border exchanges and the interplay between regional and global factors reveal how Europe's trajectory [5], particularly its divergence between East and West, fits into a larger global framework. This divergence, especially in the Cold War context, highlights the influence of international actors such as the United States and the Soviet Union. The Soviet Union's adherence to a communist economic regime significantly slowed the progress of Eastern European countries, leaving them lagging behind their Western counterparts [6].

In the broader context, globalization can be understood as a dynamic process that integrates nations and people into larger systems over time, dissolving traditional barriers. The most interesting aspects of globalization can be observed at the intersections of global processes and their local manifestations. Central to globalization are international trade, economic cooperation, and the evolution of political structures. While international exchange has always been present historically, the Cold War in Europe can be viewed as an integrative process that laid the groundwork for globalized development after 1989. In this sense, this chapter explores the causes, challenges, and effects of European integration after WWII, focusing on the key economic, political, and social factors that have influenced the globalization process.

2. The formation of economic collaborations

In historical research, there are different and competing attempts to explain the origins of globalization, with some pointing to the nineteenth century. While Iván Tibor Berend suggests that the roots of globalization in Europe can be traced back to the early modern period, when worldwide trade networks began to take shape [4], a different position presents Kevin Hjortshøj O'Rourke arguing that Europe's journey toward globalization started in the second half of the nineteenth century [1]. However, although the Cold War accelerated significant economic, political, and social transformations that elevated Europe's global position, many of these developments had already been set in motion. Even before this period, modern capitalism had already manifested through economic trade, migration, and capital investment. Following Alfred Eckes, countries such as the Netherlands, France, Switzerland, Germany, Britain, and Sweden were major contributors to foreign investments. By 1914, European companies accounted for an impressive 76.9% of the world's foreign direct investment (FDI) stock, highlighting the extent of Europe's integration into international trade long before the onset of World War II [3]. This indicates that global economic engagement patterns were well established before the major geopolitical shifts of the twentieth century.

Europe had long led the global economy, primarily due to the United Kingdom's industrial advancements during the first wave of globalization from the nineteenth to the early twentieth century. However, due to World War II, a new power emerged to lead the global economic order. As Klaus Larres asserts, the United States became "the only country which benefited from World War II, both economically and in terms of its global standing and immense military power" ([7], p. 1). For approximately 25 years after the war, Europe entered a period of defensive recovery, allowing the U.S. to temporarily take over as the leader of the global economic system [3]. This shift was mainly due to the catastrophic state of Europe after the war. As a result, both capitalist and socialist economies saw significant growth from 1944 to 1973, with disparities emerging as the USSR and Eastern Europe faced economic challenges compared to the booming Western economies [8].

In 1944, the Bretton Woods Conference created the International Monetary Fund (IMF) and the World Bank [9]. These institutions aimed to stabilize the global economy, promote international trade, break economic barriers between nations, and foster global economic interdependence. At the same time, the U.S.'s military power and economic strength solidified its position as a superpower, one that would provide significant aid for Europe's reconstruction efforts. The Marshall Plan (1947) was a significant initiative to aid European countries in various ways, including economic reconstruction and democratic re-education, particularly in Austria, Italy, and especially divided Germany. The aid provided under the Marshall Plan played a crucial role in rebuilding infrastructure, revitalizing industries, and stabilizing the economies of nations in desperate need of support. The U.S. provided Europe with $13 billion in aid and encouraged the transaction of goods between European and American industries [10]. Beyond the economic recovery, however, the plan had a profound security impact [11], as it contributed to the consolidation of trade within two distinct spheres of political influence: the Western and the Eastern.

As the Western allies identified the immediate security threats—specifically the potential resurgence of a revisionist Germany or Japan—occupation regimes were established in both countries with no definitive timeline for withdrawal. Initially, the United States announced plans to remove most of its forces from Europe within 2 years. However, the growing influence of the Soviet Union in the East and the escalating ideological tensions altered this course of action [12]. As a result, learning from its post-World War I mistakes, the U.S. became more involved in European affairs [7]. In this context, within the ideological boundaries of the consolidating capitalist Western bloc, the creation of the European Economic Community (EEC) in 1957 was a critical transformative moment that kick-started Europe's economic journey to the modern single market. The EEC aimed to create a common market where goods, services, capital, and people could move freely across borders [13]. These developments indicate a trend toward a more globalized world. The ideological opposition, however, became a significant obstacle in Europe's path toward economic integration. Ideological divisions prevented European nations from adopting a collective identity, which, as Akira Iriye suggests, is essential for successful globalization. Globalization is based on the idea that nations become progressively less important in a globalizing world [11]. Ideological considerations heavily influenced global institutions. The World Bank, for example, assisted nations in their development and, in doing so, sought to prevent them from falling under Soviet or Chinese influence. This ideological bias limited the ability of global institutions to act as neutral entities that could support and foster worldwide economic integration.

While post-World War II Western Europe experienced economic growth driven by the liberalization of trade and the creation of common markets [10], Europe under communist regimes saw limited integration into the global economy. This led to economic stagnation and inefficiencies, particularly after the failure of economic institutions like Comecon [1]. The Council for Mutual Economic Aid (Comecon) was an economic cooperation organization headquartered in Moscow, established in 1949, along with other communist satellite states in Europe, such as East Germany, Romania, Hungary, Czechoslovakia, Poland, and Bulgaria, as a direct response to Western European integration. Comecon was also an ideological project meant to showcase the advantages of socialism, emphasizing cooperation and highlighting its member states' planned economy and technological development. The Soviet Union aimed to create a unified economic system in Eastern Europe to maximize efficiency despite limited support from the local population, especially from satellite countries, which had historically developed conservative structures where landowners and the church held significant power. For the satellites, the transition to communism and a planned economy was a radical shift. Nonetheless, to control resources and coordinate industrial and agricultural production, this approach was intended to strengthen the socialist economic model and make the region more self-sufficient, reducing its dependency on the capitalist West. Although the Eastern Bloc was centrally controlled, Eastern integration was not successful, and Comecon was essentially a meaningless organization [14].

One of Comecon's problems was that the Soviet planned economy lacked traditional market forces, was highly protectionist, and placed a high value on self-sufficiency, making it more challenging to trade and further integrate with other Comecon countries. Traditionally, the Eastern Bloc countries in Comecon traded with the West but were forced to trade eastward with the Soviet Union. In the early 1950s, the

Eastern Bloc experienced economic success. There was a strong focus, with around 75–90% of all industrial investments directed toward heavy industry, and they managed to maintain economic growth for a limited time [1]. They could sustain this focus through a centrally planned economy by allocating resources to heavy industry, something that a market economy could not achieve to the same extent, as it could not concentrate so many resources on a single sector of the economy. However, this focus waned with the technological advancements and growth of the West. The Eastern Bloc struggled to keep up with consumer goods, leading to the "kitchen war." The "kitchen war" exemplified the difference between a capitalist economy and a planned economy, where the market model incentivized the development and improvement of kitchen consumer goods. As a result, Western consumers had access to dishwashers, freezers, refrigerators, and other kitchen appliances, while kitchen products in socialist countries were of inferior quality.

In line with the ideological background of Comecon, it had to ensure the transfer of technological knowledge to improve the efficiency of the Eastern Bloc's economy, which led to the establishment of international research institutions, such as the Joint Institute for Nuclear Research in 1956 and the Institute for Standardization in 1962. However, technological development in the Soviet Union achieved mixed results. While the Soviet Union excelled in areas like physics, it lagged in consumer technology, particularly computer technology. One contributing factor was the focus on developing technology cost-effectively, which often had unintended negative consequences. Additionally, the lack of encouragement for collaborative research efforts and the narrowness of professional communities further hindered technological progress in specific sectors. As Elena Kochetkova points out, another major problem was the rigid bureaucracy combined with the absence of market mechanisms. This led to the misallocation of resources, production surpluses in some areas, and chronic shortages in others. Additionally, the goal of standardized solutions was imposed on all member countries, regardless of their specific economic or social contexts. The result of planned economies and integration with Comecon countries failed, leading to social unrest in the Soviet Union and the Eastern Bloc, as the gap between living standards and economic stagnation grew [15].

Globalization went hand in hand with the rise of neoliberal economics and laissez-faire individualism, which emerged in the mid-1970s [1]. Neoliberal thinkers argued that the government's role should be to protect individual freedom, free markets, and competition [1]. However, the collapse of the Bretton Woods international monetary system in 1971 created an economic shift in Europe from a system that opted for fixed exchange rates to one that introduced floating currencies not nominally backed by a commodity such as gold or silver. Their value was solely due to confidence in that value. This pivotal moment spurred European countries to revise their policies in the 1980s, leading to a decline in state interventionism and an increase in deregulation and privatization [1]. These steps initiated a united effort to promote European economic integration and facilitated more efficient international trade and investment. Over the next 20 years, strengthening the German mark, Dutch guilder, and Swiss franc significantly accelerated globalization by "fuelling a surge in overseas investment," particularly with the U.S. [6]. This surge helped move Europe toward greater economic interdependence as traditional economic barriers began to break down. Furthermore, the formation of the European Community in 1973 further challenged U.S. supremacy in international trade, as the Western bloc eventually created a single European market, facilitating the free movement of capital [16]. This integration led to the creation of a large, unified economic area comparable to the U.S.

Economic integration in Europe, however, was not achieved until the early 1990s, despite being a gradual process throughout the post-World War II era. Divided Europe did not become genuinely globalized until the collapse of the Soviet Union and the dissolution of the East and Western blocs [16]. The creation of the European Union (EU) and the integration of the single market marked a significant turning point. For the first time since WWII, European countries were collectively motivated by the economic benefits of shared sovereignty and the establishment of supranational institutions [17]. By 1993, establishing the single market removed internal barriers. It permitted the free movement of goods, services, capital, and labor, creating a large, efficient economic area while effectively integrating Europe and creating new kinds of permeable national borders [18]. Additionally, creating a customs union eliminated internal tariffs and standardized external tariffs for non-member countries, promoting internal and external trade and, in consequence, solidifying the EU's position in the global economy.

The end of the Cold War marked a significant shift as Eastern European economies transitioned from centrally planned systems to market economies, integrating into the global economy. Economic reforms and foreign direct investment (FDI) were eagerly embraced, and many Eastern European nations subsequently joined the EU. For example, Poland's economic transition led to GDP growth and increased trade with Western Europe [19]. The diffusion of technology and innovation also boosted productivity and contributed to economic modernization.

However, globalization also introduced competition from emerging markets, leading to industrial decline in traditional sectors. The introduction of the euro and deeper economic integration within the EU created both opportunities and vulnerabilities. The financial crisis of 2007 exposed the structural weaknesses of the Eurozone's interconnected economy [20]. Globalization exacerbated disparities, sparking debates over balancing economic openness with protectionism to safeguard jobs and social welfare [21]. Moreover, globalization has deepened economic inequalities in Europe through the uneven distribution of its benefits and opportunities. Western European countries like Germany and France have experienced economic growth due to increased trade and investment, while Eastern European states like Romania and Bulgaria have faced stagnant wages and job displacement [22]. The integration of global markets has benefited skilled labor and capital owners, resulting in substantial income disparities. Furthermore, the increased mobility of capital and labor within the EU has intensified competition, undermining job security and social protection in less competitive economies [20].

3. Political interactions

The new political order in Europe after the end of World War II resulted in the establishment of two blocs. As part of this process, the U.S. and Western Europe began to view the nations of communist-dominated but non-Soviet Europe— Poland, Hungary, Czechoslovakia, East Germany, Romania, Bulgaria, Albania, and Yugoslavia—as a unified "bloc," which eventually became known as "Eastern Europe." As Appelbaum points out, this term is political and historical rather than geographic, as it does not include "eastern" countries such as Greece, which was never a communist state [11]. Nor does it encompass the Baltic States or Moldova, which, although historically and culturally similar to Eastern Europe, were fully incorporated into the Soviet Union during the Cold War. Following the Cold War, Eastern Europe had very little in common, and before 1945, the nations had never been unified in any significant way. Since 1989, the eight Eastern European nations have taken very different paths. However, between 1945 and 1989, they shared many commonalities, particularly in their political and economic experiences under communism. While there are similarities between the experiences of the Baltic States and Poland, there were also key differences: for the Baltic States, Sovietization meant the complete loss of even nominal sovereignty. The political consolidation in the West was interwoven with the economic consolidation already described above. However, beyond the existing security threats and tensions on both sides echoing the tensions between the U.S. and the Soviet Union, the political priorities shifted toward human rights and cooperation, which may be viewed as a result of "nations becoming less relevant" and a growing emphasis on international organizations [16]. A key ideological conflict between the East and West during this period centered on human rights. The Western bloc, led by the U.S., emphasized human rights as a fundamental principle and used it to criticize the Soviet Union's authoritarian regime and lack of political freedoms.

These new objectives were championed by international organizations that emerged from the geopolitical landscape of globalization and the erosion of national borders. A notable example of this focus on human rights was the World Population Conference held in Bucharest in 1974. The adoption of the World Population Plan of Action at the conference demonstrated Europe's commitment to addressing global socioeconomic issues, particularly in developing countries, on an international level. This highlights how globalization amplifies political issues, transforming domestic concerns into international challenges and emphasizing the need for collective global action in response.

The Helsinki Accords of 1975 represented another significant development during the Cold War. They emphasized human rights, economic cooperation, and security in Europe [10]. Although the accords eventually faltered, they succeeded in compelling the Soviet Union to acknowledge and respect universal human rights in Eastern Europe. This suggests that globalization had a positive effect on Europe by fostering and normalizing cooperation between the blocs. Additionally, following World War II, European nations experienced a period of decolonization. The colonial empires of Europe, including the British Empire, once dominant global powers, faced a rising wave of demands for independence. The United Nations (UN) supported this push for sovereignty by establishing the Special Committee on Decolonization (C-24) in 1961, which aided former colonies in transitioning to independent nations. Europe's approach to decolonization contributed to a relatively swift global process. The "Wind of Change" speech by British Prime Minister Harold Macmillan to the Parliament of South Africa in 1960 encapsulated this position, as the British government expressed its acceptance of growing national consciousness and indicated no intent to resist the independence of its territories [15].

Despite these official positions, some European attempts continued to exert influence over former colonies through mechanisms such as the British Commonwealth or by rebranding Portuguese territories as overseas provinces, entering the realm of neocolonialism. Nevertheless, it was clear that the world had been swept by a "wind" of independence. This wave of decolonization significantly expanded the membership of global institutions like the UN, growing from 51 member states in 1945 to 193 in 2023. While this shift allowed former colonies to participate in international geopolitics, many struggled with political and economic instability, lacking the necessary infrastructure. This led to ongoing conflicts and corruption, particularly in Africa. The continued presence of UN peacekeeping forces, such as in the Democratic

Republic of Congo [23], underscores that post-colonial politics have created new dependencies on global institutions.

Geopolitical factors at the end of the Cold War significantly contributed to the globalization of Europe by promoting economic integration, political stability, and regional cooperation. The collapse of the Soviet Union, coupled with EU expansion and NATO security, collectively facilitated Europe's deeper integration into the global economy, driving the globalization process [6]. Although economic and technological reforms during the post-World War II era indicated a gradual movement toward a global and unified Europe, full integration was not realized until the fall of the Soviet Union. Until the 1990s, a clear political divide remained between the West and the East.

Overall, the collapse of the Soviet Union was a major catalyst for collective European globalization. Some scholars point to the end of the Cold War as marked by Gorbachev's failure to revive socialism, which unintentionally steered the country toward a free-market economy [6]. Others argue that the fall of the Berlin Wall was both a physical and symbolic end to the Cold War, as it reunited two parts of Europe (East and West) after 50 years of division [24]. German unification serves as a prime example of how geopolitical developments impacted globalization in Europe [24]. In the post-Cold War era, Germany and Eastern European states joined international organizations such as the European Union. However, this development was made possible due to the collapse of the Soviet Union, which allowed for greater European unity. As countries became increasingly interconnected, governments were compelled to consider international, regional, and global dynamics, further driving the forces of globalization [6]. Moreover, to strengthen the newly established democracies with fragile structures, the EU Commission proposed agreements in 1990 with Poland, Hungary, and Czechoslovakia, offering support for democratic transitions and frameworks for trade relations [24]. This extension underscores the EU's role in promoting political and economic stability. It also reflects a broader shift, where nations are becoming "less relevant units in a globalizing world" [16], with a greater emphasis placed on global organizations such as the EU, the World Trade Organization, and the International Monetary Fund.

Moreover, the struggle for human rights transcended the ideological battles between East and West. As Iryie points out, the fall of the Soviet bloc, which ushered in a wave of freedom and democratization, should not be viewed solely through the lens of East-West confrontation. Human rights must be seen as a broader issue that, throughout history, has united the world in its pursuit of ending oppression. He encapsulates this viewpoint by asserting, "The Cold War is a footnote in the history of globalization" [16]. While this perspective is compelling, it is crucial to recognize the end of the Cold War as a significant turning point in Europe's globalization journey. The collapse of the Cold War's spheres of influence was instrumental in shaping a united Europe and reshaping Europe's governance structures, policymaking approaches, and international relations. The most significant impact has been the creation of the EU. This supranational organization has economically and politically integrated member states, harmonized laws and regulations, and developed a unified political landscape [25].

In this context, it can be argued that the development of transnational political movements is also a consequence of globalization. The EU has facilitated the rise of transnational political movements that address issues transcending national borders. For example, the European Green Parties have gained momentum by advocating for environmental policies across member states [26]. This does not contradict Iriye's argument about the role of human rights and environmentalism in shaping modern globalization [16]. Rather, it acknowledges how the end of the Cold War and the creation of the EU were pivotal in amplifying the effects of globalization, making Europe more interconnected and outwardly engaged on the global stage.

At the same time, globalization has fueled populist movements that criticize the erosion of national sovereignty and the rise of economic inequality. Initially, many older works, such as Egan [25], praised the EU for creating a unified political landscape. However, recent developments reveal a more complex reality. Parties like the National Front in France challenge the pro-globalization consensus. The Brexit referendum further illustrates this trend, with Britain voting to leave the EU to regain control over national laws and borders [27]. This wave of nationalism has polarized European politics as nations become increasingly reluctant to relinquish their national identities despite growing interconnectedness.

Furthermore, the world seems to be returning to pre-Cold War divisions in recent years. The ongoing conflict in Ukraine is a prime example of this shift. The war has triggered a re-evaluation of dependence on global supply chains, particularly in the energy sector. Nations are now seeking to become more self-sufficient and less interdependent, even within the EU. This conflict has prompted countries to reassess their trade relationships and alliances, challenging the principles of open markets and free trade that underpin globalization [28]. These developments highlight the complex interplay between regional conflicts and global economic policies.

4. Technological innovation

Technological change played a crucial role in driving globalization in Europe after World War II. From the 1950s, technology rapidly expanded from military and scientific applications to commercial uses [2]. These advancements not only facilitated economic integration but also profoundly challenged and transformed European societies. Key technological innovations included advancements in transportation, communication, and industrial development. The Marshall Plan (1948–1952) provided critical financial aid to Western European countries, fueling economic recovery and technological advancement. This led to significant investments in infrastructure, and industries such as aerospace, automotive, and electronics flourished, with companies like Airbus and Volkswagen emerging as global leaders. The post-war era saw rapid advancements in telecommunications, exemplified by developments in radio and television technology. The emergence of computers began in the 1950s, with countries like the UK leading in early computing technology (e.g., the development of the Ferranti Mark I). In consequence, Western Europe witnessed a boom in consumer electronics in the 1960s and 1970s. Innovations in home appliances and entertainment systems enhanced the quality of life and sparked consumer culture.

In terms of collaboration, however, John Coatsworth reevaluates these early postwar years as a time of lost opportunities for US-USSR cooperation, pointing to the current state of the art that questions whether any were realistic. Considering Stalin's Soviet policy, his suspicion of Western leadership, and American military-industrial interests, historians have become more skeptical about the chances of European alignment in the 1940s. Soviet power rested in its ideological appeal and postwar prestige based on the communist transformation from a weak Russian empire that had collapsed before the German onslaught in World War I into a powerful state that played the leading role in defeating Germany in World War II. However, the Red

Army's enormous size, while an important factor, is not the only aspect explaining the Soviet victory. The technological advancements in some crucial areas of military production ensured the Soviets' technical superiority over the Germans. Additionally, Soviet universities and institutes were deeply integrated into society and produced some of the greatest European scientists. In 1945, when Stalin demanded a crash program to develop a nuclear weapon, he succeeded in achieving this within 5 years [8]. The Soviet Union's early successes in the space race were crucial. Eastern European nations contributed to space technology, with Hungary and Poland advancing satellite technology. However, the Eastern Bloc faced challenges due to technological isolation and limited access to Western innovations. This resulted in inefficiencies and lagging consumer technology compared to the West. The launch of Sputnik 1, the world's first artificial satellite, triggered the establishment of NASA and the space race, and it took another 18 years until Europe signed the commitment to space exploration and technology in 1975, when the European Space Agency (ESA) was founded.

Research and development also involved military advancements. One of the most groundbreaking achievements of the technological race was the development of the Internet and satellite communication systems in the U.S. The launch of the Advanced Research Project Agency Network (ARPANET) in the 1960s, which eventually evolved into the modern Internet, opened the gateway for real-time information exchange across continents [29]. Communication technology should ensure secure information in case of a nuclear strike. However, the technological improvements also affected other sectors of everyday life, such as transportation [30].

The end of the Cold War marked a significant turning point for technological integration. The collapse of the Iron Curtain allowed for increased technological exchange between East and West following years of struggle in Eastern Europe [31]. During the Cold War, the lack of technological integration in the East led to inefficiencies and often inaccurate information sharing [15]. For instance, when Soviet experts visited Romania to learn about papermaking, they found Romanian methods to be less efficient and outdated compared to their own [15]. The Eastern Bloc was in a state of technological stagnation, with satellite states struggling to share knowledge effectively across borders. The fall of the Soviet Union was pivotal in reintegrating Eastern Europe with the more technologically advanced West. This reintegration reduced the costs of cross-border transactions, promoted cultural exchange, and fostered economic interdependence, laying the foundations for the modern globalized world.

One way Europe revised its policies was through a strategic increase in funding for research and development, which rose from 5.4 billion ECUs in 1990–1994 to 12.3 billion ECUs by 1994–1998 [1]. This fostered greater cooperation among leading global businesses. However, the modernization of industries in Europe occurred at varying speeds depending on the country. According to Kearney's globalization and internationalization index, Western European countries such as Britain, France, the Netherlands, and Denmark ranked among the global top 10 by 1990, while Hungary, Poland, and other Eastern European nations only managed to catch up in the second half of the 1990s [1].

This suggests that while technological advancements fueled globalization in Europe, its full realization could not occur until the political turmoil and divisions subsided at the end of the Cold War. Additionally, improved communication enabled Europe to revise its policies and enhance cross-border coordination, promoting greater economic interdependence [2]. The invention of the Internet, the proliferation of communication satellites, fiber optics, and the World Wide Web introduced new concepts of "collectivity, instantaneity, and punctuality" [2].

A positive outcome of enhanced communication across borders was the reduction of transportation costs. However, Hyung-Gu Lynn notes that while the transportation of goods increased, it did not necessarily lead to higher levels of integration in Europe when compared to pre-1914 levels [2]. In parallel, O'Rourke argues that the Industrial Revolution of the eighteenth century had a profound impact on transportation, as the advent of steam technology introduced new methods for intercontinental trade by both sea and land [1]. Although innovations in transportation were significant in the pre-war period, the scale and speed of mass transportation in the post-war era triggered a new revolution that was crucial for achieving globalization. This reinforces the argument that while globalization is a gradual historical process, it was not fully realized until after World War II. For instance, the cost of air transportation decreased throughout the 1960s, further driving and accelerating global trade [2]. The U.S. set a precedent with the Airline Deregulation Act of 1978, which liberalized domestic air travel and international cargo flights, eventually influencing Europe. This not only expanded global trading networks but also led to an increase in long-term migration as crossing borders became cheaper and faster than ever before.

Considering the Cold War as a time period, the political climate influenced technological priorities. While Western Europe thrived on consumer-driven innovation and collaboration, Eastern Europe focused on military and heavy industrial technologies. This led to significant achievements but also notable limitations. The end of the Cold War eventually led to a convergence of these technological paths as Eastern Europe sought to modernize and integrate into the global economy.

5. Cultural and social effects of globalization

Global processes manifested locally throughout the Cold War era and continue to do so, particularly in cities, which serve as nodes for economic, political, and various social activities [32]. However, in historical research, significantly less emphasis is placed on the cultural effects and impacts that cultural and social aspects may have on globalization [33].

The Cold War and rapid globalization in Europe have facilitated the movement of people, contributed to cultural diffusion, and led to increased cultural exchange. Migration reached unprecedented levels during the twentieth century. While emigration rates from Europe were already significant in 1911, at 14 percent, migration from less-developed to more-developed countries within Europe has also become a new phenomenon [34]. This trend is closely linked to both labor and political migration, the use of technological innovations, and advancements in commercial flights that have reduced the cost and time of travel, making longer-term migration more accessible [2].

The rapid welfare increase in Western Europe was built on migrants. Different professional groups in the West, such as Greeks and Italians, contributed to various Western European industries as early as the 1950s, stimulating industrial growth and laying an important milestone for the development of post-war welfare. The need for migrant labor and migrants' integration into the European market clarifies that citizenship and urbanization are not isolated phenomena but are deeply interconnected with global economic, political, and cultural systems. In contrast, Eastern European countries operated under centrally planned economies, which prioritized heavy industry and military technology over consumer goods. Significant investments were made in sectors like energy production and defense technology, with notable achievements in nuclear energy and missile technology. Education in science and engineering was emphasized, leading to strong accomplishments in theoretical physics and mathematics.

To meet the demands of growing mass consumption, increasing populations, and expanding industries, international organizations were prompted to collaborate in addressing these challenges. Consumerism has driven the development of a new lifestyle that has evolved in parallel in both the East and the West, although it is characterized by similar patterns to some extent. The youth of the 1970s and 1980s in Europe sought to drink Coca-Cola, wear jeans and polo shirts, and listen to The Beatles. The difference was that in the West, these goods were openly accessible, while in the East, they were restrictively distributed through special retail chains that sold them in dollars as foreign currency. Moreover, environmental issues have gained prominence on the global agenda, particularly since the 1970s. The first UN Human Environment Conference, held in Stockholm, brought together environmental groups and NGOs to tackle these concerns collectively [2]. The oil crises of the 1970s focused attention on energy consumption and dependence on fossil fuels, while incidents such as the 1976 Seveso disaster in Italy, where a chemical leak exposed residents to dioxins, highlighted the dangers of industrial pollution and galvanized public concern. Activism began to grow as citizens became more aware of pollution, deforestation, and the impacts of industrial activities on health and ecosystems. In response to these growing concerns, European countries started to implement environmental regulations. The European Community established several directives aimed at pollution control and conservation, laying the groundwork for future environmental policies. International cooperation on environmental issues in the 1980s led to conferences such as the 1982 World Charter for Nature and the 1987 Montreal Protocol, which aimed to address ozone depletion.

Globalization brought interconnectedness but also created disparities, as the global is deeply intertwined with the local. This emphasizes that globalization is not a universal phenomenon but one shaped by place, time, and context. Birgitta Svensson highlights cities as a focal point where global processes take on distinct local forms [32]. Cities act as arenas where global movements and transformations occur, impacting local lives and influencing broader global trends that can be represented in evolving subcultures, changing food habits, clothing styles, or shifting patterns in growing multicultural class societies. In this way, urban areas become focal points for understanding the complexities of identity, citizenship, and the challenges posed by an interconnected world.

The end of the Cold War and the establishment of the Schengen Area in 1995 formally created a framework for the free movement of people within Europe [35]. Borders have become less rigid, and terms such as European mobilization have been politically promoted, granting individuals greater freedom of movement. This increased mobility has further extended cultural diffusion, facilitating the exchange of traditions, languages, and customs from different parts of the world [34]. In this process, the relationship between national states and cities illustrates how globalization and urbanization have evolved together, creating a complex interplay that shapes modern society. In this changing landscape, the nature of national citizenship evolves in a globalized world, bringing forth tensions between cultural identity and universalist principles.

Culturally, globalization has facilitated the blending of traditions, with Western consumerism spreading across Europe post-1989, as evidenced by the rise of the single market and the Schengen Agreement, which allowed for the free movement of people and ideas. However, the simultaneous rise of neo-tribalism and fundamentalism, driven by feelings of alienation, has fueled a backlash against this cultural integration. Many, particularly the "new middle class," face the uncertainty and fear associated with the rapid pace of globalization. As Zygmunt Bauman suggests, globalization has fostered divisions as much as connections, reinforcing inequalities through uneven access to mobility and resources. While a globalized elite enjoys the privileges of free movement and transnational networks, much of the local population remains tied to their specific geographic and social contexts, experiencing the harsh consequences of globalization without its benefits. Consequently, he argues, being "local" in a globalized world has increasingly come to symbolize social deprivation and degradation [36]. Bauman cautions against viewing globalization as a homogenizing force for humanity, as its consequences are wide-ranging, from the shifting dynamics between labor and capital to the criminalization of poverty under consumerism [36]. Following Bauman, globalization should not be confused with the idealistic aspirations of universalization. While universalization seeks to create a global order aimed at improving life and fostering justice, globalization, in contrast, centers on the present—on the lived experiences of people today.

6. Conclusions

After World War II, the convergence of economic integration, technological advancement, and political decisions played a crucial role in shaping Europe's path toward globalization. Moreover, different countries dealt with wartime collaborators and established new political orders to prevent past errors, often emphasizing unity over individual accountability. While some researchers point to the roots of globalization, this contribution argues that the end of the Cold War and the collapse of the Soviet Union ultimately enabled full-scale globalization in Europe. The collapse of the Soviet Union, the creation of international institutions such as the IMF, the World Bank, and the European Union, along with technological innovations like the Internet and high-speed rail networks, facilitated Europe's integration into the global economy. The political unification through the formation of the EU provided the framework for member states to harmonize laws, foster collective identity, and form transnational political movements. Economically, the single market enhanced Europe's competitiveness and connected the economic and labor markets, yet also revealed economic disparities, particularly between Eastern and Western Europe, that, although smudging, still persist as a heritage of the Cold War era.

The Cold War divided Europe, giving rise to distinct Eastern and Western blocs. Analyzing the divergent development paths and how they were significantly shaped by the Soviet Union's influence on European affairs during the Cold War is a valuable contribution to the concept of global history, which challenges the traditional notion of Western civilization. The Soviet Union's commitment to maintaining a communist economic regime severely hindered the progress of Eastern European countries, causing them to fall behind their Western counterparts. Additionally, the current state of research, supported by multi-archival studies, helps to transcend the East-West division and elevate the perspective from below, considering the needs of people that also contributed to ongoing change. This aspiration for welfare in households throughout Europe is one aspect that explains the widespread political interest in social policy at the time, driven by poverty and the general devastation of lives and social security experienced during World War II.

When considering whether a united Europe or the desire for economic advantages was the driving force, it seems that both factors played a role. One crucial reason for integration in the early stages was the desire for reconstruction and the establishment of institutions that would prevent another war. In 1945, 73% of the French population supported the idea of a union. The countries that were less interested in this, led by the United Kingdom, formed EFTA. Over time, national considerations gained greater importance, as evidenced by France's boycott of meetings due to dissatisfaction with self-interest issues. It was during periods of economic hardship that a common market (SEA) was established, eventually leading to the creation of what we now know as the EU—an example of successful integration. While the idea of a united Europe was central to the formation of the EC, subsequent developments have increasingly been driven by economic self-interest. Additionally, when considering the aspect of social welfare, one might argue that the integration processes in both Eastern and Western Europe during the Cold War were driven by similar objectives. Both blocks endured widespread devastation following World War II and recognized that deeper integration could foster peace and stability. However, political divisions based on ideology, lifestyle, and ethnicity intensified in the 1970s, leading to rising social tensions.

Additionally, integration was seen as a way to enhance the efficiency of their respective economies. In Western Europe, integration facilitated greater competitiveness for European products, making trade across borders easier and promoting economic growth. Conversely, the Eastern Bloc, operating under Comecon, lacked the market mechanisms and incentives to compete with the global market. This resulted in more isolated and less efficient economic systems, further hindering their ability to achieve the level of economic development witnessed in the West. The post-war integration in Eastern Europe and the organization Comecon did not survive the dissolution of the Soviet Union. It was a vastly different organization from those in Western Europe and was largely controlled by the Soviet Union. Following James Libbey, Comecon was not established to create a common market but rather as a means of waging economic war against Yugoslavia [14]. Trade flows that had previously gone westward were redirected to the East. The organization evolved over time, and perspectives on trade shifted after Stalin's death. In the debate over whether ideological or national goals were prioritized, it appears that both played a role. Ideology was significant in the cooperation between organizations, emphasizing equality over competition, even though this hampered collaboration. The Soviet Union's interest in Western technology, along with Comecon's increasing trade with the West, demonstrates that ideology did not always dominate decision-making. Individuals also found ways to exploit opportunities and circumvent restrictions imposed by ideological foundations.

By the end of the twentieth century, Soviet dominance in Eastern Europe had come to an end, and Europe opened up for liberal consolidation. Politically, the formation of the EU unified member states, harmonized laws, and fostered a collective identity while also giving rise to transnational political movements that addressed global issues. Economically, the single market drove growth and helped integrate Europe's previously divided economic and labor markets. However, it also exacerbated economic inequalities and exposed vulnerabilities. The free movement of people and goods enriched Europe's diversity but also brought new challenges. Economic disparities between Western and Eastern Europe highlight the uneven distribution of benefits. Additionally, the rise of populist movements underscores the tension between national sovereignty and global integration. Conflicts such as the Ukraine war have prompted a re-evaluation of reliance on global supply chains and challenged the principles of a globalized open market. As globalization evolves, Europe must navigate these complexities to maintain its global prominence and address socioeconomic and political challenges.

Globalization is a dynamic, synergistic process that, over time, integrates people and nations into larger structures and communities while dissolving traditional barriers [5]. Following the fall of the Berlin Wall in 1989, Europe was able to deepen its interconnectedness and interdependence—defining characteristics of globalization. The fall of the Iron Curtain marked a new era of cultural exchange across Europe, characterized by the homogenization of cultural elements, notably the widespread adoption of Western consumer goods. The single market enabled Eastern European countries to access previously inaccessible Western products. The Schengen Agreement further enhanced this exchange by allowing free movement across borders, facilitating cultural diffusion as people migrated throughout Europe [37]. Globalization has also brought Asian, American, and African cultures into Europe through various channels, including food, music, and technology [38]. Consequently, Europe has become a hub of diverse cultures. However, this cultural diffusion encounters resistance in various national and local contexts.

While modern developments may appear novel in scale, they are rooted in long-standing patterns of social interaction and community formation. As research points out, globalization experiences suffer from periodic reversals, raising questions about whether technological and political advancements can sustain continuous progress [1]. Brexit, for example, challenges the strength of European unification and integration, as the United Kingdom's withdrawal from the European Union represents a shift away from interconnectedness. The rise of nationalism may suggest that individual nations are increasingly prioritizing independence and moving away from the ideals of globalization [33]. Furthermore, the effects of economic inequality, environmental degradation, and a rising wave of populism and nationalism show that conflicts like the Ukraine war trigger a re-evaluation of global dependencies, particularly regarding energy and supply chains, raising questions about the principles of free trade and interconnected markets.

Author details

Izabela A. Dahl
School of Humanities, Education and Social Sciences, Örebro University, Sweden

*Address all correspondence to: izabela.dahl@oru.se

IntechOpen

© 2025 The Author(s). Licensee IntechOpen. This chapter is distributed under the terms of the Creative Commons Attribution License (http://creativecommons.org/licenses/by/4.0), which permits unrestricted use, distribution, and reproduction in any medium, provided the original work is properly cited.

References

[1] O'Rourke KH. Europe and the causes of globalization, 1790 to 2000. In: Europe and Globalization. London: Palgrave Macmillan UK; 2002. pp. 64-86

[2] Lynn H-G. Globalization and the cold war. In: Immerman R, Goede P, editors. Oxford Handbook on the Cold War. Oxford: Oxford University Press; 2013. pp. 584-601

[3] Eckes AE Jr. Europe and economic globalization since 1945. In: Larres K, editor. A Companion to Europe Since 1945. Chichester: Wiley Blackwell; 2009. p. 249

[4] Berend IT. Globalization: Return to laissez-faire? In: An Economic History of Twentieth-Century Europe: Economic Regimes from Laissez-Faire to Globalization. Cambridge: Cambridge University Press; 2006. pp. 263-326

[5] Zemon Davis N. Global history. Many stories. In: Kerner M, editor. Eine Welt. Eine Geschichte? München: Oldenbourg Verlag; 2001. pp. 373-380

[6] Guyatt N. The end of the cold war. In: Immerman R, Goede P, editors. Oxford Handbook on the Cold War. Oxford: Oxford University Press; 2013. pp. 605-622

[7] Larres K. Introduction. In: Larres K, editor. A Companion to Europe Since 1945. Chichester: Wiley Blackwell; 2009

[8] Coatsworth J et al. Cold wars and hot wars: Economic boom and slowdown 1950-1985. In: Global Connections: Politics, Exchange, and Social Life in World History. Vol. 2. Cambridge: Cambridge University Press; 2015. Since 1500

[9] Woods N. The International Monetary Fund and World Bank. In: Encyclopedia of Government and Politics. London, New York: Routledge; 2013. pp. 953-968

[10] Jackson I. Economic developments in Western and Eastern Europe since 1945. In: Larres K, editor. Companion to Europe Since 1945. Wiley-Blackwell; 2009. pp. 95-112

[11] Applebaum A. Iron Curtain: The Crushing of Eastern Europe 1944-1956. London: Allen Lane; 2012

[12] Horowitz S. Restarting globalization after world war II. Comparative Political Studies. 2004;**37**(2):127-151

[13] Pinder J. Federalism and the beginnings of European Union. In: Larres K, editor. A Companion to Europe since 1945. Wiley-Blackwell; 2009. pp. 35-44

[14] Libbey J. CoCom, Comecon, and the economic cold war. Russian History (Pittsburgh). 2010;**37**(2):133-152

[15] Kochetkova E. Technological inequalities and motivation of soviet institutions in the scientific-technological cooperation of Comecon in Europe, 1950s–80s. European Review of History: Revue européenne d'histoire. 2021;**28**(3):355-373. DOI: 10.1080/13507486.2020.1835829

[16] Iriye A. Historicizing the cold war. In: Immerman R, Goede P, editors. Oxford Handbook on the Cold War. Oxford: Oxford University Press; 2013. pp. 15-31

[17] Dinan D. European integration: From the common market to the single market. In: Larres K, editor. A Companion to

Europe Since 1945. Wiley-Blackwell; 2009. pp. 133-150

[18] Allen C, Gasiorek M, Smith A. The competition effects of the single market in Europe. Economic Policy. 1998;**13**(27):440-486

[19] Gros D, Steinherr A. Economic Transition in Central and Eastern Europe: Planting the Seeds. Cambridge: Cambridge University Press; 2004. DOI: 10.1017/CBO9780511805646

[20] Wyplosz C. The six flaws of the Eurozone. Economic Policy. 2016;**31**(87):559-606

[21] Sapir A. Globalization and the reform of European social models. JCMS: Journal of Common Market Studies. 2006;**44**(2):369-390

[22] Dumont M, Stojanovska N, Cuyvers L. World inequality, globalisation, technology and labour market institutions. International Journal of Manpower. 2011;**32**(3):257-272

[23] Murphy R. UN peacekeeping in the Democratic Republic of the Congo and the protection of civilians. Journal of Conflict and Security Law. 2016;**21**(2):209-246

[24] Germond C. The end of the cold war and the unification of the European continent. In: Larres K, editor. A Companion to Europe Since 1945. Blackwell: Wiley; 2009. pp. 208-227

[25] Egan M. Constructing a European Market: Standards, Regulation, and Governance. Oxford: Oxford Academic Press; 2001. DOI: 10.1093/0199244057.001.0001

[26] Bomberg E. The Europeanisation of green parties: Exploring the EU's impact. West European Politics. 2002;**25**(3):29-50

[27] Inglehart R, Norris P. Trump, Brexit, and the Rise of Populism: Economic Have-Nots and Cultural Backlash (Working Paper No. RWP16-026). Harvard University, Harvard Kennedy School; 2016. DOI: 10.2139/ssrn.2818659

[28] Cafruny A, Fouskas VK. Ukraine, Europe, and the re-routing of globalization. Journal of Balkan and Near Eastern Studies. 2024;**26**(1):1-22

[29] Leiner BM, Cerf VG, Clark DD, Kahn RE, Kleinrock L, Lynch DC, et al. A brief history of the internet. ACM SIGCOMM Computer Communication Review. 2009;**39**(5):22-31

[30] Bonnafous A. The regional impact of the TGV. Transportation. 1987;**14**(2):127-137

[31] Grix J. Towards a theoretical approach to the study of cross-border cooperation. Perspectives. 2001;**17**:5-13

[32] Svensson B. Globaliseringens många ansikten. In: Sjöberg M, editor. En Samtidig Världshistoria. Lund: Studentlitteratur; 2014. pp. 1023-1036. DOI: 10.1163/187633110X494661

[33] Lieber RJ, Weisberg RE. Globalization, culture, and identities in crisis. International Journal of Politics, Culture, and Society. 2002;**16**:273-296

[34] Fischer S. Globalization and its challenges. American Economic Review. 2003;**93**(2):1-30

[35] Flockton C. Economic integration since Maastricht. A companion to Europe since 1945. In: Larres K, editor. A Companion to Europe Since 1945. Blackwell: Wiley; 2009. pp. 270-301

[36] Bauman Z. Globalisation. The Human Consequences. London: Polity; 1998

[37] Makosa PM. Emigration of poles to the United Kingdom: History, present state and future prospects. International Migration. 2018;**56**(5):137-150

[38] Shimemura Y. Globalization vs. Americanization: Is the world being Americanized by the dominance of American culture. Comparative Civilizations Review. 2002;**47**(47):7

Chapter 4

Perspective Chapter: Brexit, Emmanuel Macron and the Resurgence of the *Europe puissance*

Glenn Wasson

Abstract

Tensions on continental Europe have become more pronounced in recent years following the United Kingdom's departure from the European Union. Brexit required a reorientation of the European Union. With the aim of challenging German leadership of the EU, French President Emmanuel Macron revived the Gaullist *Europe puissance* – the concept of a European military entity to rival the superpowers on the international stage. Macron – a critic of Brexit and NATO – wanted a common defense policy for Europe, which guarantees 'strategic military sovereignty.' This chapter will examine two themes. Firstly, the proposed EU restructuring as a competitor of NATO will be discussed to discover the military threats of a *Europe puissance* when Putin's Russia looked to expand its borders into Ukraine. Furthermore, the decline in Franco-German relations will be investigated since Macron's concept provoked backlash from German leaders and EU Commission President Ursula von der Leyen. Exploring the Europe puissance allows us to ascertain the divisions between EU partners when NATO became Europe's voice in geopolitical matters.

Keywords: European Union, Emmanuel Macron, military sovereignty, supranational, common ambition

1. Introduction

On 25 April 2024, French President Emmanuel Macron gave a speech at La Sorbonne, which attracted the attention of many domestic journalists present. It did not, however, cause much consternation outside of France despite its inflammatory rhetoric. Macron said 'We are at a tipping point, and our Europe is deadly. It's just up to us' [1]. The two-hour long speech referred to Macron's grand design for the European Union in military and geopolitical terms. He continued 'The *Europe puissance* is simple, it makes itself respected and ensures its security' [2]. The *Europe puissance* is a concept that has taken on many different guises since French Prime Minister Guy Mollet first proposed it in November 1956. The timing of the *Europe puissance* proposal is very important to contextualizing the concept in geopolitical history. The Mollet government decided to pursue the construction of a European superpower (*Europe puissance*) as a means of counteracting France's imperial decline, which the failed Franco-British intervention in the Suez Canal in October 1956 only served to exacerbate. The British acceptance of a cease-fire on 6 November 1956 further embarrassed France, and forced the Mollet government to reorientate its defense policy towards its European Community (EC) partners. Mollet's vision for a *Europe puissance* contained the integration of EURATOM – the EC vehicle for nuclear cooperation and collaboration through a Franco-German *Comité militaire et technique* [3]. Thus, one aspect of the *Europe puissance* remains constant: the inclusion of European supranational frameworks for the construction of a new superpower to disrupt the existing bipolar world order. This was certainly Mollet's intention in 1956, and also that of his successors with French President Charles de Gaulle seeking to augment France's position on the world stage by proposing the French nuclear deterrent as the base for a *Europe puissance* during the 1960s.

Macron's vision for a *Europe puissance* follows the same line of continuity as his predecessors. In 1953, French Prime Minister Pierre Mendès France argued against the creation of a European defense network, stating that it would undermine efforts towards European integration in the energy and economic sectors. However from 1956 to the mid-1960s, the *Europe puissance* became an *en vogue* concept. During this period, there were several concepts for European defense being discussed. NATO reforms were high on the European defense agenda. President de Gaulle offered a more nuanced alternative of European defense planning, which augmented the share of control that EC member states would have on the continent. De Gaulle's *Europe puissance* existed as a means for France to challenge the bipolar order and reassert the world power role, which was diminished because of the Suez Crisis [4]. For European Community countries, European defense philosophy in the post-Suez period centred on the separation of continental military decision-making from US management. France and the Federal Republic of Germany (FRG) sought to exert some degree of independence over their defense policies, and openly criticized Britain for holding to their previous status as a Great Power and not adapting to the new bipolar order, with their acquiescence to US dominance in the West [5]. German Foreign Minister Franz Josef Strauss disapproved of Britain's post-Suez posturing on the European continent, going as far as critiquing Her Majesty Queen Elizabeth II's visit to France 'as dwelling on the past glories of the *entente cordiale* rather than on the new European philosophy.'

Much of the academic work has centred on French leaders' failed attempts at cultivating the Five European Community nations into accepting a *Europe puissance* – de Gaulle's alternative to NATO and the WEU. For instance, Douglas T. Stuart has argued that the French desired this alternative avenue for European defense as it offered a way to exert control over military affairs on the continent. Stuart's argument, among others, has concentrated on the incompatibility of French foreign policy and US control within the Atlantic Alliance command structure. The crux of this argument can be found in the United States' treatment of France during the Suez Crisis, since the former was coerced 'to choose between its African vocation and its friendship' [6].

In the broadest sense, it is well-known that the *Europe puissance* grew from a lack of acceptance over US domination in European defense decision-making. The concept has taken on many forms since the Suez Crisis and has, most recently, been revived to act as a military wing for European Union during the Iraq war and later following Britain's withdrawal from the European Communities framework [7]. However, any examination of the *Europe puissance* must consider the changing dynamics of the political landscape. This chapter seeks to understand how Emmanuel Macron has revived the *Europe puissance* to maintain French influence in the current geopolitical climate. In particular, this chapter will discuss the ongoing conflict in Ukraine and how Macron's proposal for a revived *Europe puissance* was not compatible with the resurgence in NATO's significance. In addition, the chapter will also investigate how the French government used the *Europe puissance* as a potential power grab in the wake of the United Kingdom's departure from the European Union in December 2021. In doing so, this chapter will argue against Galtung's analysis that the EU was a 'capitalist superpower', particularly when referring to geopolitical defense matters [8].

2. Brexit and the reorientation of the European Union

On 26 September 2017, Emmanuel Macron stood up at the Université de la Sorbonne to make a speech on his future grand design ideas for the European Union. It is noteworthy that this speech came four months after his inauguration as French President and set the tone for the guiding principles for his tenure. He began his speech thusly:

> *I have come to talk to you about Europe. "Again", some might exclaim. People will just have to get used to it, because I will not stop talking about it. Because this is where our battle lies, our history, our identity, our horizon, what protects us and gives us a future [9].*

Macron's speech laid bare his political ambitions for his European partners to see. He referenced the advent of the migrant crisis and the growing 'nationalism, identitarianism, protectionism [and] isolationist sovereignism' in EU member states as issues which France needed to combat. The solution to those crises was the Macronian *Europe puissance*. However, this new French grand design idea was not completely predicated on the maintenance of a nuclear deterrent akin to its predecessors. The Macronian initiative required the establishment of an *armée européenne* to ensure European autonomy where its security and global influence is concerned. Jacques Delors had previously recommended an *Europe puissance* during his tenure as EU Commission President, describing the creation of such a project as a new 'hardcore' proposal for the preservation of the European Communities [10].

The revival of the *Europe puissance* can be traced to the resurgence of disruptive forces on continental Europe. The annexation of Crimea in February and March 2014 created a tense atmosphere between European nations and the Russian Federation. The threat of expansionist nations on continental Europe and the marked decline of democratic institutions in nations of strategic importance caused Macron to revive the Gaullist grand design idea. He stated in his speech 'a European Union reinvented in this way is a precondition for their not turning their backs on Europe and moving towards either Russia or Turkey, or towards authoritarian powers that do not currently uphold our values' [9]. The French President's desire for reform of the European Union into a more secure and autonomous geopolitical institution has received much attention from academics. In the context of Russia and Turkey's departure from the expected democratic norms of the post-Cold War period, Soli Özel has argued that the 'post-national, liberal… project of European integration is in a profound crisis' since nations on the near-exterior of the EU have been openly challenging the founding principles of the Community project [11]. Indeed in 2016, Turkish President Recep Tayyip Erdoğan adopted a Eurasianist approach with the aim of becoming an influential power in the Middle East. The Eurasianist approach was Erdoğan's attempt to challenge the bipolar order in the Middle East by establishing itself as an 'order setter' in the region. In addition, Turkey experienced a turbulent

– albeit short – military coup against the Erdoğan regime in July 2016. The state's move towards soft authoritarianism was the rationale for the army's revolt. The failed coup unironically led to the purge of 45,000 education workers, generals, military personnel and several governors which served to enhance Erdoğan's reputation as a quasi-dictator [12]. Erdoğan's move towards authoritarianism represented the deep divide between the EU and Turkey in the post-Arab Spring period, especially in relation to the NATO command structure. Turkey's strategic position on NATO's southern flank accompanied by Russia's expansion in the Crimea required the strengthening of Europe's military complex [13]. Macron's *Europe puissance* was considered the appropriate alternative to the weakening of NATO. French politicians of the Gaullist tradition expressed unwavering support for the Macronian grand design idea. Xavier Bertrand, the leader of the Conservative party *Nous France*, praised Macron's desire to strengthen the French military hardware complex through the development of France's nuclear energy manufacturing. Bertrand described France's atomic energy production as 'une énergie d'avenir' [14].

The support from right-wing French politicians made Macron's case for European sovereignty over military decisions easier to fight, particularly during a period of great uncertainty for the European project. On 23 June 2016, the United Kingdom of Great Britain and Northern Ireland, and Gibraltar took to the polls to vote on their continued membership of the European Union. The result has become a source of much controversy and continues to plague British politics to this day. With 52 per cent of the votes, the United Kingdom's future outside of the European Union was secured. However, this left the EU in a quasi-identity crisis. Former French President de Gaulle had once argued that France needed intra-European relations to succeed if she was to remain in the 'front rank' of world affairs, something he demanded given that, in his view, 'France cannot be France without greatness' [15]. Thus, the United Kingdom's departure from the EU framework caused a power imbalance within the Communities since the UK was the third largest financial contributor to the Union. Macron – an uncompromising critic of both Brexit and NATO – stated that he wants a common nuclear policy for Europe, which guarantees 'strategic military sovereignty'. In addition, the French President also stated that Brexit was a 'mistake', and that Britain must pay for turning its back on the 'common ambition' of the European Union [16]. The Brexit vote signaled a positive outcome to right-wing political movements across Europe. In France, the negotiations surrounding the United Kingdom's departure from the European Union ran in parallel with the rising popularity of the *Rassemblement Nationale* (RN), which has seen its share of the Presidential election vote increase from 33.9 per cent in 2017 to 41.45 per cent in 2022 [17]. Indeed, RN Party President Marine Le Pen has reflected the impacts of Brexit in the formulation of her policies. For the 2017 Presidential Election, her guiding policy was to protect 'France's national sovereignty in a Europe of independent nations at the service of its peoples' [18]. The policy shares similarities to the Leave campaign's landmark slogan of 'Take Back Control' during the Brexit referendum, according to Helen Drake [18]. The possibility of a so-called 'Frexit' placed pressure on Macron to ensure that his grand designs for closer fiscal and military cooperation within the structure of the EU became a reality.

The success of the Brexit campaign laid bare the inadequacies of the EU to maintain its present structure. Policies regarding strict legal and economic frameworks have emboldened populists across continental Europe. Macron's proposals for strict budgetary requirements – namely, increases – following the British withdrawal from the EU highlighted the fragility of France's position within the Community's leadership. In March 2018, Macron set out economic reforms in the National Assembly as a means of steering France to a position of budgetary security in the eyes of its European partners. Macron's reforms were a geo-political necessity given German Chancellor Angela Merkel's outright rejection of his economic outlook for the EU. Following Macron's accession to power in July 2017, he proposed a radical transformation of the European economy – one relying upon a resurgent labour market supported by favorable EU-wide state pension systems. However, Merkel's Christian Democrats (CDU) vetoed the idea, principally as Macron did not command support from many of his contemporaries from other political groups [19]. The French workers' unions, the Confédération Générale du Travail (CGT) and the Confédération Française et Démocratique du Travail (CFDT), resisted Macron's economic reforms as the decentralizing of the work force would ultimately weaken their members' right to protest – an essential facet of the French *grévoculture* [19].

German resistance to Macronian initiatives also impacted negatively on the *Europe puissance* idea. Macron's economic and cultural liberalism was a public humiliation on the continental stage. Between 2017 and 2020, the French economy experienced a significant decline of eight per cent following the Yellow Vest protests and the advent of the Covid-19 pandemic lockdowns [20]. Fabian Escalona has argued that the decline of national unions and the loss of French monetary independence in the public sphere deteriorated France's ability to manipulate the direction of travel within the European Union [20]. Additionally, Britain's withdrawal from the European Union left the Community without its key strategic guide within the Common Security and Defense Policy (CSDP), given that the United Kingdom only contributed 2.3 per cent of its forces to the Communities' mission preparation [21]. Thus, Macron vigorously argued in favor of institutionalizing the *Europe puissance* as a necessary addition to the CSDP following the United Kingdom's departure. The *Europe puissance* was characterized as an important augmentation of the existing European Union framework. Merkel and the current President of the European Commission Ursula von der Leyen were originally suspicious of Macron's model for the *Europe puissance*. In the case of von der Leyen, she supported the idea of a European security network, which looked towards cultivating new bonds with partner nations in the Indo-Pacific. The rationale for von der Leyen's alternative was the growing threat of China to nations around the world, something she said was paramount given the 'considerable damage' a 'simple laptop can cause' [22]. Von der Leyen also called for a supranational *Europe puissance*, rather than a French-led organization proposed by Macron. The EU Commission President's alternative focused on the cultivation of multilateral projects of 'common European interests' [23]. Thus, Macron's *Europe puissance* would have struggled to gain traction with Community partners since it did not have the support of its current leadership.

The French proposal for a *Europe puissance* also failed to overcome German objections. The Federal Republic of Germany (FRG) has a historical precedent for rejecting multiple iterations of the *Europe puissance*. Following German Chancellor Konrad Adenauer's agreement with de Gaulle to institutionalize Franco-German relations in the context of European integration, the 1963 Élysée treaty created a bilateral axis within the European Communities where France would lead defense preparations as a prelude to the creation of a *Europe puissance* [24]. As a key player in central Europe, Germany has found itself torn between two different defense grand design philosophies since the 1960s. Firstly, West Germany had benefitted from close alignment with NATO from 1955, which included membership of the Western European Union (WEU). The foundational principle of the *Europe puissance* proposals of de Gaulle's tenure reflected the geopolitical realities of the period. De Gaulle wanted to use France's growing nuclear weapons capability to create a European military superpower, with the intention of challenging the existing bipolar framework consisting of NATO and Warsaw Pact countries under the leadership of the United States of America and the Soviet Union. It was the nuclear element that weakened any chance of the first *Europe puissance* proposal being accepted. The FRG's membership of the WEU also constrained its ability to lead de Gaulle's *Europe puissance* as the Control of Fissile Materials agency ensured that it was unable to use any nuclear components for the purposes of national defense [25, 26]. Leadership in Europe was an important concept for Germany throughout the Cold War period following a resurgence in their economy during the late-1960s. Germany's alignment with NATO ensured its incorporation into US grand design proposals, such as the ill-fated Multilateral Force (1962–1966). Adenauer's successor Ludwig Erhard later clarified that while the FRG would still consider assigning forces to the Multilateral Force, Franco-German cooperation was the most effective means of ensuring that the West German people would 'have the right to self-determination' [27].

Subsequently, the German position on leadership of the European Communities has been more entrenched over the ensuing decades. As the 1980s progressed, West German Chancellor Helmut Kohl professed of a Germany that would acquire a leadership role within the existing European framework. Kohl stated that the new Germany, which he envisaged would rise post-reunification, would be 'built under a European roof' [28]. Kohl's portrayal of Germany as a European nation suggests a slight departure from his predecessor's direction of travel. This characterization of Germany as a leader in Europe provoked much concern in France. French historian Pierre Guillen has previously warned that a unified Germany with its growing technological and economic power, its geographical position and sizeable population had 'a power which will upset the balance in Europe and which will ensure it a quasi-hegemony' [29]. In many ways, academic discourse has debunked the fears of Guillen and his contemporaries. Ulrich Krotz argued that the Élysée Treaty demarcated a new 'special relationship' between both European nations [30].

The re-emergence of Germany as a political actor on the European stage hindered the development of the Macronian *Europe puissance*. Indeed, one of the main German objections to the proposal centred upon nostalgia. The Macronian *Europe puissance* – while an advancement of the single-mindedly nuclear powered, Gaullist alternative – still maintained some of the themes which led to the failure of its previous iterations. The former Permanent Representative of France to the EU Pierre Sellal identified German objections as a 'certain mistrust' of partner nations, particularly France which would lead the proposed superpower [31]. Suspicion of fellow European partners is nothing new, with historical precedents set before the foundation of the European Coal and Steel Community in 1952. In fact, the French government had increasingly found itself isolated on the European stage because of its persistence with previous iterations of the *Europe puissance* idea. Germany's attitude to increasing its defense role with European partners has focused primarily on strengthening the Atlantic Alliance. For instance, in 1969, months before de Gaulle's resignation as French President, Germany and the United Kingdom opted to create a *contre-coalition* designed to support the Benelux Plan – a proposal conceived by Pierre Werner, the Prime Minister of Luxembourg, with signatories signaling their support for the creation of a Europe economic and monetary union (EMU) by 1979 [32]. A Germano-British coalition severely undermined any hope of the French President's proposal for a *Europe puissance*, which by 1969 had been adapted to include a Free Trade Agreement with member states, from achieving any success. The British took concrete steps to subvert the French proposals [33]. The majority of EEC and partner nations accepting the Benelux plan highlights the increasing isolation which the French government experienced because of its commitment to the *Europe puissance*. Progressively this isolation has been reflected in academic discourse. Coralie Delaume argued that the *Europe puissance* proposal, regardless of its interpretation, cannot achieve success given that by its very nature, it would create a *contre-coalition* against the existing NATO command structure designed to oversee the defense of continental Europe [34].

The historical precedents concerning the failure of the *Europe puissance* idea reflect the current geopolitical climate. Macron's desire to revive the *Europe puissance* has met with a similar lack of success as its predecessors. General historical trends of bipolarity have thwarted French governments in establishing the *Europe puissance* as a credible defense alternative. For example, in 1973 the superpowers' move towards nuclear non-proliferation further eroded the *Europe puissance*'s chances of success. While Britain received upgraded Polaris technology, it came at the cost of strict adherence to the Strategy Arms Limitation Treaties, thus limiting any potential counter-balance a *Europe puissance* could manifest against Soviet aggression and ensuring US defense hegemony in Europe remained [35].

3. The resurgence of NATO and the postponement of the *Europe puissance*: for now

The perceived failures of the Atlantic Alliance as an organization responsible for the coordination of European defense matters were one of the catalysts for the Macronian *Europe puissance*. Macron could not have been clearer in his Sorbonne speech of September 2017 that, in his eyes, the European Union would become a competitor for NATO in the military sphere. Indeed, the perceived rapprochement with Germany over defense matters resulted in a renewal of Franco-German relations. While she was critical of his economic policies, Merkel supported the idea of a revived *Europe puissance* given the increasing demand of the CSDP following the United Kingdom's impending departure from the EU. Merkel considered the 'narrow confines' of the CSDP restrictive to Germany's influence within the wider sphere of European defense [36]. Thus, closer ties and negotiations between Germany and France between 2017 and 2019 evolved into a renewed bilateral agreement. On 22 January 2020, the French President and the German Chancellor signed the Aachen Treaty, on the 56th anniversary of the ratification of the Élysée Treaty. The timing of this bilateral agreement was noteworthy as both countries agreed to revive promises within the Élysée Treaty. France and Germany agreed to strengthen cybersecurity, defense against autocratic regimes (in this case Russia) and cooperate over civil engineering projects. However, one discreet facet of the Aachen Treaty was the decision to strength a Franco-German voice within the European Union. The creation of a new Franco-German axis in the European Communities owed much to the advent of Brexit and Donald Trump's US presidency. Macron emphasized France's role within a strategically autonomous European Union as a key to the resurgence of the *Europe puissance*. The presidency of Donald Trump contributed to France acting more unilaterally on the European and international stage. Following Trump's election, the French government concentrated its defense spending on preparations for investing in EU military matters [37]. Furthermore, Macron also used Trump's introduction into geopolitical affairs to discredit his right-wing opponents. Known Eurosceptic and President of *Rassemblement National* Marine Le Pen, who criticized Macron's *Europe puissance* concept and vigorously defended the early actions of the Trump presidency, was charactised as a Trump 'apostle' for declaring that the 'EU is dead, but does not know it yet' on the day of his inauguration [37].

In addition, the introduction of Trump caused a profound North-South split among EU partners. The growing presence of right-wing governments in European governments resulted in European integration in military terms being even harder to achieve than before the Brexit referendum. For instance, Italian Prime Minister Giorgia Melloni has recently committed her country to the priorisation of European defense within the framework of the Atlantic Alliance. In a speech to the Italian Parliament, she clearly stated: 'it is Italy's duty to fully contribute, because [...] freedom has a cost and that cost, for a nation, is its ability to defend itself and prove it is a reliable partner within the framework of alliances to which it belongs' [38]. The Italian Prime Minister's bold declaration of her – and her country's – Atlanticist credentials highlights the growing divide between the Franco-German axis within the EU and other member states. Her role as President of the 'soft' Eurosceptic European Conservatives and Reformists Party further demonstrates the growing split between European leaders around the proposed defense of Europe. Macron hoped that the *Europe puissance* would gain traction among his European partners. However, the rise of right-wing parties in positions of power across Europe, in particular Italy and Hungary has led to a loss of interest in continental defense being constructed from within the European Communities.

The divisions between EU member states has been epitomized in recent years by Emmanuel Macron's inflammatory comments about the future of NATO. On 21 October 2019, in an hour-long interview with *The Economist* in the Élysée Palace, President Macron delivered a stark warning to his European allies – mainly, that they cannot rely on the United States any longer for leadership on defense matters. He stated bluntly 'What we are currently experiencing is the brain death of NATO' going further to warn that the European Union stands on 'the edge of a precipice' [39]. The stark warning concerning NATO was a response to the fledgling *Europe puissance* concept. Macron's grand design for Europe was in a slow decline with his beating of the drum for European defense integration falling on deaf ears. In particular, several EU states had recently begun to prioritize Euro-Atlantic defense. Between 2017 and 2023, Finland, North Macedonia, Montenegro and Sweden had joined the Atlantic Alliance with existing member states committing to undertake military deployments in the face of a growing threat from Russia. Macron questioned whether NATO as an organization was still committed to the principles of collective defense following the United States' withdrawal from northern Syria [40]. His comments drew criticism from his closest allies. Merkel disagreed, describing his words as 'drastic.' Despite the disapproval of France's Aachen Treaty partner – and perhaps more shockingly – the Putin government welcomed Macron's comments, describing them as 'truthful words' [40]. Macron's comments went against the whole character of the Atlantic Alliance. Article Five of the NATO Charter guarantees the 'collective defense of territory' under the control of member states [41]. Macron's use of the US withdrawal from Northern Syria as criticism for the Atlantic Alliance was unfounded considering that the area was not under total US control. Furthermore, the Syrian matter highlights the deepening divisions between the US and France which prompted Macron's criticism. The French government favored a political settlement led by direct involvement from the international community in accordance with the United Nations Security Council Resolution (UNSCR) 2254, which the Trump administration openly disregarded through its withdrawal from Northern Syria without prior consultation with NATO allies. In particular, the French government upheld the importance of 'reaffirming its strong commitment to the sovereignty, independence, unity and territorial integrity of the Syrian Arab Republic' while 'urging all parties to the UN-facilitated political process to adhere to the principles identified by the International Syria Support Group' [42].

Macron's attempts to focus the international conversation around the 'brain death' of NATO were ill-timed. In 2018, NATO Secretary General Jens Stoltenberg, the President of the European Council Donald Tusk and EU Commission President Jean-Claude Juncker signed the Joint Declaration on Cooperation. Article Nine of the Declaration guarantees that both parties' 'mutually reinforcing strategic partnership contributes to strengthening security in Europe and beyond' [43]. Going further the Declaration reads:

> NATO and the EU play complementary, coherent and mutually reinforcing roles in supporting international peace and security. We will further mobilize the combined set of instruments at our disposal, be they political, economic or military, to pursue our common objectives to the benefit of our one billion citizens [43].

It is the assurance that both the European Union and the Atlantic Alliance will contribute to the advancement of international security which undermines any fundamental progress for the Macronian *Europe puissance*. The Declaration also contained evidence of pre-existing military cooperation between NATO and the EU, which further demonstrates the lack of need for a *Europe puissance*. Article Eleven states 'We have reached tangible results in countering hybrid and cyber threats, operational cooperation including maritime issues, military mobility, defense capabilities' [43]. Between 2016 and 2018, the European External Action Service (EEAS) was the epicenter for 74 joint actions between the EU and NATO. While these joint operations laid the foundations for the Joint Declaration in 2018, they papered over the cracks in the multilateral relationships between transatlantic partnerships [44]. The move towards greater unity in defense matters between NATO and the EU has greatly mitigated against the impacts of the Brexit process. Macron's comments about the decline of NATO did not have the intended impact. The implementation of a *Europe puissance* now looks quite unlikely. However, this was not always the case in the immediate aftermath of the Brexit vote. Sir Robin Niblett, the former director of Chatham House and specialist on international relations, had previously stated that 'France has seen itself as the policy leader of the EU', and with the United Kingdom's absence from the EU framework, 'Mr Macron is acting with too heavy a hand' [45]. Nevertheless, the growing amity between the EU and NATO has stifled any appetite for competition. The departure from 'Great-Power' competition, which has experienced a resurgence following the Cold War, has been a welcome development in fostering stronger relations between NATO and the EU. The ratification of a bilateral relationship between both organizations has successfully quelled the desire for further competition over defense matters on the continent.

The Russian invasion of Ukraine on 24 February 2022 proved to be the final nail in the coffin of the *Europe puissance*. On 3 March, Russian Foreign Minister Sergey Lavrov argued that intervention into Ukraine was essential to Russia's strategic interests considering 'the threat to the lives of citizens of the Russian Federation'. He submitted a petition to the UN General Assembly proposing the use of 'armed forces of the Russian Federation on the territory of Ukraine until normalization of the sociopolitical situation in that country.' Interestingly, Lavrov's rhetoric follows similar patterns to the backlash to Russia's annexation of Crimea in 2014 [46]. The reaction of the international community to Russia's false determinations of self-defense was one of overwhelming support for Ukraine. Both NATO and the EU have either began or continued the process of making Ukraine a member of their organization. Since the 2006 Bucharest Summit, NATO has worked with Ukraine on the road towards membership. In fact, In September 2020, Ukrainian President Volodymyr Zelenskyy approved a National Security Strategy with the aim of advancing his country towards full integration with NATO [47]. Arguably, this is part of the reason behind Russia's invasion considering the growing Atlanticist influence within Eastern Europe, with its nearest neighbor Poland already being a member of the Alliance.

Similarly, the EU has opened its doors to Ukraine following the invasion, with the country formally announcing its application on 28 February 2022. It was not until December 2023 that the EU decided to open accession negotiations with Ukraine on its role within the European Union with the first intergovernmental conference for negotiations occurring in June 2024. Now, the Russian invasion of Ukraine marked a significant turning point for discussions around the idea of a *Europe puissance*. The North Atlantic Council twice held consultations between members of NATO and the EU. The results were decisive. Since Ukraine was not a NATO member state, Atlantic Alliance forces could not intervene directly under the terms of Article Five of the NATO Charter. However, Article Five of the Washington Treaty guarantees the protection of 'all Allies', which gave NATO member states the pretext to begin openly supporting the Ukrainian war effort with military hardware and armed forces staff for training purposes. As of the end of March 2022, 40,000 troops from NATO's Very High Readiness Joint Task Force (VJTF) stand ready on its Eastern Flank. In addition, all Allied member states have strengthened the Forward Presence battlegroups based in Bulgaria, Hungary, Romania and Slovakia, in case of Russian advance towards Allied territory [48]. The concentration of the NATO allied forces on the situation in Ukraine circumvented any discussions around the future defense of the European Union. Nevertheless, the growing support from NATO member states, including France, for the Ukrainian war effort is not the most mitigating piece of evidence for the collapse of the *Europe puissance* idea. In January 2022, the French government, in conjunction with the commanders of its armed forces, decided to take up the leadership role of the VJTF, with the aim of restoring its credentials as a leader on the European stage – an idea that has been progressively weakened during Macron's tenure. NATO Secretary General Stoltenberg praised Macron's government for renewing its interest in Alliance activities. He said, 'the Very High Readiness Joint Task Force is a substantial contribution to our collective defense, and France's leadership is a strong display of commitment and capabilities' [49].

Macron's turn towards NATO has only continued in step with the war in Ukraine. France has only recently hit its target of spending two per cent of Gross Domestic Product on NATO defense projects, a statutory aim for all members of the Atlantic Alliance. Despite ceding control of the VJTF in January 2023, France has continued its contributions to collective defense by stationing more troops on NATO's Eastern Flank, principally in Romania and Estonia. Following a meeting between Macron and Stoltenberg in Paris on 24 June 2024, the Secretary General praised France's role in NATO aviation and maritime defense particularly in the Baltic regions. Stoltenberg was categorical in his praise: 'French naval ships keep our sea lanes open and safe' [50]. The icing on the cake for Stoltenberg was the French decision to guarantee NATO access to its nuclear force – the *force de frappe* – as a condition for the overall security of the Atlantic Alliance. In many ways, the prominent role France plays in NATO's response to the war in Ukraine highlights how the European security order has changed in 'ways unseen since the end of the Cold War'. France's departure from desiring a forcibly generated leadership role within a *Europe puissance* has shown

Perspective Chapter: Brexit, Emmanuel Macron and the Resurgence of the Europe puissance
DOI: http://dx.doi.org/10.5772/intechopen.1006487

Macron's willingness to adapt politically and maintain his nation's strategic position within Europe, which was coming under increasing threat the longer he persisted with his revived notion of a European superpower within the EU.

4. Conclusion

The *Europe puissance*, at least for the moment, is confined to the annals of history once again. The advent of the war in Ukraine has proved to be the final nail in the coffin for what was designed to return France to the 'front rank on the international stage' [51]. Despite a lack of success for the Macronian *Europe puissance*, the French President stated in October 2022 that a common defense policy was essential to protect France's 'vital interests' after Russian President Vladimir Putin's threat of atomic weapons use returned the question of nuclear non-proliferation to the fore [52]. Nevertheless, the medium through which this common defense policy would now take shape was the Atlantic Alliance. The whirlwind story of the *Europe puissance* from possible renewal and rebirth during Macron's Sorbonne speech to the French President's recommitment to playing a leadership role in NATO demonstrates the controversial nature of the concept in a bipolar framework. For example, the lack of support from France's traditional ally Germany, coupled with the reticence from EU leaders to adopt such a military plan, illustrates that the *Europe puissance* in the Macronian guise only succeeded in achieving the same as its predecessors and divide the opinion among European leaders. The French objective remains to create a common defense policy among partners. What has changed since 2017 is the extent of the partnership, shifting from a strictly European collaboration to a broader Euro-Atlantic community with 23 nations now meeting the commitment to contributing two per cent of GDP to NATO defense projects [53]. Thus, while the departure of the United Kingdom from the European Union presented an opportunity for Macron to reclaim a leadership role in Europe for France, the *Europe puissance* concept contained the same issues which plagued the previous models – namely, the renouncing of European dependence on the United States and the lack of a supranational element, which hampered Franco-German relations during Erhard's tenure. Thus, Macron's turn towards European defense within the framework of the Atlantic Alliance is a welcome one given the current geopolitical uncertainties following Russia's invasion of Ukraine.

Author details

Glenn Wasson
Campbell College, Belfast, Northern Ireland

*Address all correspondence to: gwasson03@qub.ac.uk

IntechOpen

© 2024 The Author(s). Licensee IntechOpen. This chapter is distributed under the terms of the Creative Commons Attribution License (http://creativecommons.org/licenses/by/4.0), which permits unrestricted use, distribution, and reproduction in any medium, provided the original work is properly cited.

References

[1] Catherine Nay. Moi, president d'une Europe "puissance"?, Valeurs [Internet]. 2024. Available from: Catherine Nay: Moi, président d'une Europe "puissance" ? - Valeurs actuelles [Accessed: May 06, 2024]

[2] Le Figaro. Emmanuel Macron prône une "Europe puissance" qui "se fait respecter" et "assure sa sécurité". [Internet]. 2024. Available from: Emmanuel Macron prône une «Europe puissance» qui «se fait respecter» et «assure sa sécurité» (lefigaro.fr) [Accessed: May 06, 2024]

[3] L'épilogue de la crise de Suez, qu'il n'était plus question qu'ils prétendent jouer dans la cour des grands. see Crémieux, A. Vers une Europe-puissance; Comment aboutir concrètement à l'Europe de la défense. Paris: Éditions L'Harmattan; 2020. pp. 27-28

[4] Decup SM. France-Angleterre; Les relations militaires de 1945 à 1962. Paris: Haute Études Militaires; 1998

[5] Gordon PH. Charles de Gaulle and the nuclear revolution. In: Gaddis JL et al., editors. Cold War Statesmen Confront the Bomb; Nuclear Diplomacy since 1945. Oxford: Oxford University Press; 1999

[6] Stuart DT. The United States and NATO out-of-areas-disputes: Does the cold war provide precedents, or merely prologue? In: Schmidt G, editor. A History of NATO – The First Fifty Years. Vol. 1. Basingstoke: Palgrave Macmillan; 2001

[7] Lindley-French J. Europe Puissance or Macro-Gaullisme? Defence Synergia. Updated [Internet]. Available from: https://www.defencesynergia.co.uk/europe-puissance-or-macro-gaullisme/ [Accessed: March 08, 2021]

[8] Orbie J. A civilian power in the world? Instruments and objectives in European Union external politics. In: Orbie J, editor. Europe's Global Role; External Policies of the European Union. Abingdon: Routledge; 2016

[9] Speech by Emmanuel Macron, Université de la Sorbonne [Internet]. 2017. Available from: https://www.elysee.fr/en/emmanuel-macron/2017/09/26/president-macron-gives-speech-on-new-initiative-for-europe [Accessed: May 23, 2024]

[10] Mongrenier J-S. Souveraineté européenne, inconsequence française et defense de l'Occident. Diplomatie. 2021;**11**:62

[11] Özel S. At the End of the Day, Where Will Turkey Stand? Instituto Affari Internazionali (IAI); 2019

[12] Loveday M et al. Turkey Is Expected to Curb Military Power as Purge Expands. [Internet]. 2016. Available from: https://www.washingtonpost.com/world/turkey-jails-generals-as-post-coup-purge-widens/2016/07/19/db076c84-4d1f-11e6-bf27-405106836f96_story.html [Accessed: May 27, 2024]

[13] Wódka J, Kuźmicz S. European Union and Turkey in the post Arab spring era: Mapping strategic interests in the turbulent neighbourhood. Insight Turkey. 2013;**15**:123-140

[14] Anon. 2022: Xavier Bertrand défend le nucléaire, "énergie d'avenir" [Internet]. 2021. Available from: https://www.la-croix.com/2022-Xavier-Bertrand-defend-nucleaire-energie-avenir-2021-04-18-1301151478 [Accessed: June 04, 2024]

[15] Warlouzet L. A revival of Europe puissance? Études. 2022;**7-8**:7-20

[16] Emmanuel Macron appelle le Royaume-Uni à « choisir » sa relation avec l'UE. Le Figaro. [Internet]. 2020. Available from: https://www.lefigaro.fr/international/emmanuel-macron-appelle-le-royaume-uni-a-choisir-sa-relation-avec-l-ue-2021 [Accessed: March 05, 2021]

[17] The Party has also Achieved Significant Gains in the European Parliamentary Election during this period, see Startin, N. Marine Le Pen, the Rassemblement National and breaking the 'glass ceiling'? The 2022 French presidential and parliamentary elections. Modern & Contemporary France. 2022;**30**:427-443

[18] Drake H. France, Britain and Brexit. In: Martill B, Staiger U, editors. Brexit and beyond; Rethinking the Futures of Europe. London: UCL; 2018

[19] Tassinari F, Tetzlaff S. Rebooting the Franco-German Engine. Danish Institute for International Studies; 2017. pp. 1-5

[20] Escalona F. Le "moment Macron". Cités. 2017;**72**:175-185

[21] Bulmer S. Germany and the European Union: Post-Brexit hegemon? Insight Turkey. 2018;**20**:11-28

[22] De Meyer K. Ursula von der Leyen dessine les piliers d'une Europe-puissance. [Internet]. Les Echos. Available from: https://www.lesechos.fr/monde/europe/ursula-von-der-leyen-rend-hommage-a-la-jeunesse-et-fixe-les-nouvelles-orientations-de-lunion-europeenne-1346318. 2021 [Accessed: June 12, 2024]

[23] Nolan L. European Must 'Turbo Charge' Defence Sector – Von der Leyen [Internet]. RTÉ. Available from: https://www.rte.ie/news/2024/0507/1447845-europe-must-turbo-charge-defence-sector-von-der-leyen/; 2024 [Accessed: June 12, 2024]

[24] Soutou G-H. L'alliance incertaine; Les rapports politico-stratégiques franco-allemands, 1954-1996. Paris: Fayard; 1996

[25] Mallard G. L'Europe puissance nucléaire, cet obscur objet du désir. Critique internationale. 2009;**42**:141-163

[26] Giraud A. Construction européenne et défense. Politique étrangère. 1990;**55**:513-524

[27] Archives nationales, Communiqué franco-allemand faisant suite à la visite de Ludwig Ehrard, chancelier de la République fédérale d'Allemagne. 1963, AG/5(1)/1438

[28] Wicke C. Helmut Kohl's Quest for Normality; his Representation of the German Nation and himself. New York: Berghahn; 2015

[29] Guillen P. La question allemande; 1945 à nos jours. Paris; Imprimerie Nationale Éditions: 1996

[30] Krotz U. Three eras and possible futures: A long-term view on the Franco-German relationship a century after the first world war. International Affairs. 2014;**90**:337-350

[31] Sellal P. The groundwork of European power. Revue Européenne du Droit. Groupe d'études géopolitiques. 2021;**3**:4-6

[32] Solar PM, de Jong HJ. The Benelux countries. In: Foley BJ, editor. European Economies since the Second World War. London: Palgrave Macmillan; 1998

[33] For addition information on how the British actively thwarted French attempts at achieving a European leadership role. see Sanderson, C. Perfide Albion? L'affaire Soames et les arcanes de la diplomatie britannique. Paris: Publications de la Sorbonne; 2011

[34] Delaume C. Le couple franco-allemand n'existe pas; Comment l'Europe est devenue allemande et pourquoi ça ne durera pas. Paris: Michalon Éditeur; 2018

[35] Hynes C. The Year that Never Was; Heath, the Nixon Administration, and the Year of Europe. Dublin: University College Dublin Press; 2009

[36] Kunz B. Why Franco-German leadership on European defense is not in sight. Policy Brief. Norwegian Institute of International Affairs. 2019;**10**:1-4

[37] Shapiro J, Pardijs D. The transatlantic meaning of Donald Trump: A US-EU power audit. European Council on Foreign Relations. 2017;**232**:1-47

[38] Marrone A. The defence policy of Girogia Meloni's government: A traditional posture with a conservative tinge. Instituto Affari Internazionali. 2022;**22**:1-7

[39] Anon. Emmanuel Macron Warns Europe: NATO Is Becoming Brain-Dead. The Economists. [Internet]. 2019. Available from: https://www.economist.com/europe/2019/11/07/emmanuel-macron-warns-europe-nato-is-becoming-brain-dead [Accessed: June 26, 2024]

[40] The United States withdrew from northern Syria without prior consultation with its Euro-Atlantic allies, see Anon. Nato Alliance Experiencing Brain Death, Says Macron. BBCNews. [Internet]. 2019. Available from: https://www.bbc.co.uk/news/world-europe-50335257 [Accessed: June 24, 2024]

[41] Gardner H. NATO and the UN: The contemporary relevance of the 1949 North Atlantic treaty. In: Schmidt G, editor. A History of NATO – The First Fifty Years. Vol. 1. Basingstoke: Palgrave Macmillan; 2001

[42] UN Resolution 2254 – Middle East (Syria). Available from: http://unscr.com/en/resolutions/doc/2254 [Accessed: August 13, 2024]

[43] Joint Declaration on EU-NATO Cooperation. Available from: https://www.nato.int/cps/en/natohq/official_texts_210549.htm [Accessed: August 13, 2024]

[44] Petrov P, Schütte L, Vanhoonacker S. The future of EU-NATO relations: Doing less better. Atlantisch Perspectief. 2020;**44**:38-44

[45] Ozdemir C. The Franco-German rivalry in the post-Brexit Europe. International Relations. 2021;**18**:129-149

[46] McDermott R, Reisinger H, Smith-Windsor B. Cold War Déjà Vu? NATO, Russia and the Crisis in Ukraine. NATO Defense College; 2014. pp. 1-5

[47] Relations with Ukraine. Available from: https://www.nato.int/cps/en/natohq/topics_37750.htm [Accessed August 13, 2024]

[48] Tardy T. Ukraine, NATO and the Madrid strategic concept. In: Tardy T, editor. War in Europe; Preliminary Lessons. NATO Defense College; 2022. pp. 13-24

[49] France takes the lead of NATO's highest readiness force. Available from: https://www.nato.int/cps/en/natohq/news_190458.htm [Accessed: June 27, 2024]

[50] Remarks by Jens Stoltenbery. Available from: https://www.nato.int/cps/en/natohq/opinions_227402.htm?selectedLocale=en [Accessed: August 6, 2024]

[51] Todorov T. L'Europe puissance. Diplomatie. 2003;**6**:12-13

[52] Vincent E. Emmanuel Macron sème la doute sur la position française en case d'attaque nucléaire russe sur l'Ukraine. Le Monde. 2022. Available from: https://www.lemonde.fr/international/article/2022/10/14/emmanuel-macron-seme-le-doute-sur-la-position-francaise-en-cas-d-attaque-nucleaire-russe-sur-l-ukraine_6145786_3210.html [Accessed: May 17, 2023]

[53] Landay J, Psaledakis D, Hunnicutt T. Over 20 NATO Allies to Spend at Least 2% of GDP on Defense in 2024, Says Stoltenberg. Reuters. [Internet]. Available from: https://www.msn.com/en-gb/news/world/over-20-nato-allies-to-spend-at-least-2-of-gdp-on-defense-in-2024-says-stoltenberg/ar-BB1ooCYh?ocid=BingNewsSerp [Accessed: June 27, 2024]

Chapter 5

A Tale of Two Cities: Navigating the Politics of Hate of North Korean Migrants in Seoul and New Malden

Stella Micheong Cheong

Abstract

This chapter examines the experiences of North Korean migrants in Seoul, South Korea, and New Malden, United Kingdom, focusing on their navigation of discrimination, hate speech, and the development of peacebuilding capacities. Utilizing autobiographical narrative inquiry, the study provides a dual comparative analysis of these two cities to understand the migrants' experiences in different cultural and sociopolitical contexts. The concept of "bridging civic identities" is central and characterized by cosmopolitanism, interconnectedness, and imaginativeness, enabling the transformation of conflict-attuned civic identities into peacebuilding civic identities. In Seoul, migrants face significant discrimination rooted in the "division habitus," a legacy of the Korean War, but develop strategies to overcome these challenges, leveraging educational opportunities and social networks. In New Malden, a cosmopolitan space, migrants reconstruct new civic identities, the so-called "cosmopolitan (civic) identities" and gain skills to adapt to British society, benefiting from the social welfare system. The chapter highlights the comparative analysis of these cities, revealing how those unique Northerners transform their civic identities, the conflicts they feel with belonging, and how they cultivate new capacities as bridge citizens.

Keywords: north Korean migrants, politics of hate, bridging civic identities, peacebuilding capacities, autobiographical narrative inquiry

1. Introduction

> "It was the best of times, it was the worst of times, it was the age of wisdom, it was the age of foolishness, it was the epoch of belief, it was the epoch of incredulity, it was the season of Light, it was the season of Darkness, it was the spring of hope, it was the winter of despair"
>
> -Charles Dickens [1], A Tale of Two Cities-

The above-mentioned iconic opening line from Charles Dickens' A Tale of Two Cities resonates powerfully with the experiences of North Korean migrants in Seoul and New Malden. Just as Dickens juxtaposed London and Paris during the tumultuous period of the French Revolution, this study examines the contrasting realities faced by North Korean migrants in two distinct urban landscapes of the twenty-first century. Seoul, the bustling capital of South Korea, and New Malden, a suburban enclave in London, represent vastly different sociopolitical and cultural contexts, each offering unique challenges and opportunities for these migrants as they navigate the politics of hate in the complex terrain of integration and identity formation. While the comparison between eighteenth-century London and Paris and twenty-first-century Seoul and New Malden may seem unconventional, it highlights the enduring nature of human struggles and the resilience of the human spirit. In Seoul, North Korean migrants face a society shaped by a history of conflict and division, where they are often viewed with suspicion and hostility due to the "division habitus" ([2, 3], p. 373). In contrast, those in New Malden find themselves in a more cosmopolitan environment, offering both opportunities and challenges as they navigate the complexities of British society, often experiencing what Garapich [4] terms "hierarchies of deservingness" among migrant communities.

This chapter delves into the experiences of North Korean migrants in Seoul and New Malden, examining how they navigate the politics of hate and the development of peacebuilding capacities as bridge citizens. The central question guiding this study is how these unique migrants transform their civic identities, the conflicts they feel with belonging, and how they cultivate new capacities as bridge citizens. Key questions addressed include: How do the sociopolitical and cultural contexts of Seoul and New Malden shape North Korean migrants' experiences of the politics of hate? What strategies do these migrants employ to overcome discrimination and develop peacebuilding capacities? How do their civic identities evolve as they adapt to their new environments? Through autobiographical narrative inquiry [5, 6], the research aims to provide a nuanced understanding of the migrants' experiences in different cultural and sociopolitical contexts. By exploring these issues, the study seeks to shed light on the complex processes of identity formation and the potential for individuals to become agents of change in their communities, ultimately providing insights into the complex process of integration and identity formation among North Korean migrants in two distinctly different urban settings.

The concept of "bridging civic identities" is crucial to this study, characterized by cosmopolitanism, interconnectedness, and imaginativeness [7]. These identities enable the transformation of conflict-attuned civic identities into peacebuilding civic identities, allowing migrants to become active participants in fostering social cohesion and understanding. Through a comparative analysis of Seoul and New Malden, this study aims to reveal the strategies and resources migrants employ to overcome challenges and build new lives, ultimately contributing to a more nuanced understanding of the challenges faced by North Korean migrants and highlighting their potential as agents of positive social change. By examining the concept of "bridging civic identities" and how it manifests in different sociopolitical contexts, this research seeks to inform policies and practices that can better support the integration of North Korean migrants and other displaced populations. Furthermore, by comparing the experiences in Seoul and New Malden, this study aims to identify best practices and areas for improvement in both societies, potentially contributing to more effective and compassionate approaches to migrant integration and peacebuilding efforts.

2. Contextual background

The territorial division of the Korean Peninsula has its roots in the aftermath of World War II, when the United States and the Soviet Union agreed to divide the country along the 38th parallel for administrative purposes [8]. However, this temporary division became a permanent fixture, with the Democratic People's Republic of Korea (DPRK) in the North and the Republic of Korea (ROK) in the South claiming legitimacy over the entire peninsula, leading to the Korean War (1950–1953) [9–11]. The war resulted in the signing of the Armistice Agreement, but a formal peace treaty was never concluded, leaving the two Koreas technically at war for over seven decades [12]. The prolonged division has led to the development of unique political, economic, and social systems in each country [13–17], as well as the consolidation of distinct civic identities among their respective populations [18–21]. North Korea has developed a unique "Suryong-Dominant Party-State System" under the leadership of the Kim family, with the *Juche* ideology, which emphasizes self-reliance, serving as the ruling ideology [22, 23]. Subjects such as "Revolutionary History" are used to promote a distorted historical narrative and reinforce the regime's legitimacy [23]. In addition, the regime has employed education as a tool to systematically instill in its citizens animosity, hostility, and contempt toward capitalist South Korea and American imperialism [22–24].

In contrast, South Korea has evolved into a capitalist, democratic nation, experiencing rapid economic growth and democratization [14, 15, 25, 26]. In South Korea, education has been a key driver of economic growth and social development, but it has also perpetuated ideological divisions and anti-communist sentiments, particularly during the post-war period and military dictatorships [24, 27–29]. The National Security Law, enacted under an anti-communist framework, has cultivated a perception of North Korea as a national adversary among South Korean citizens, exacerbating ideological divisions within South Korean society and leading to discrimination against North Korean migrants [30–34]. This situation reflects the complex interplay of direct, structural, and cultural violence described by Galtung [35–37], where the territorial division and the Korean War have fixated the conflict and shaped collective identities. The seven-decade long division has resulted in the formation of a "division habitus" ([3, 38], p. 371) and internalization of "conflict-attuned civic identities" [18], embodying the hostility, structured misunderstanding, and distrust between the people of the two Koreas, in a process of identity transformation or "becoming, or avoiding becoming a certain citizen" [39]. Consequently, North Korean migrants in South Korea hold a dual status: legally, they automatically obtain South Korean citizenship, but socially, they are often stigmatized and marginalized due to their North Korean identity [10, 32, 40]. This dual status is deeply intertwined with the Politics of Hate in Korean society, rooted in the division system that has led to the development of different values, norms, and identities between the two Koreas over the past half-century [16, 30, 40].

3. Theoretical foundations: Politics of hate

The politics of hate can be understood through two primary frameworks: traditional and critical. Traditionally, the politics of hate involves inciting animosity against specific groups or individuals, often rooted in prejudice or bias, and historically used as a tool for social control or reinforcing power structures [41–44]. Aristotle's Rhetoric illustrates how hatred can be a rational response to perceived vices, embodying the traditional perspective on hate politics. In contrast, the critical politics of hate, as articulated by scholars like James and McBride [45], examines how neoliberal capitalism impacts the lived experiences of hate victims and perpetrators, suggesting that hate is deeply embedded in social and economic structures. They argue that the neoliberal capitalist framework fosters individualism and competition, benefiting the wealthy elite and perpetuating systemic hate [46].

The study of hate politics has gained significant academic attention, particularly as global migration and refugee crises have intensified. Recent research has focused on the psychological, motivational, organizational, and tactical aspects of hate, as well as its manifestations in political discourse and institutional practices [47]. This interdisciplinary approach, encompassing fields such as anthropology, law, and sociology, highlights the multifaceted nature of hate as a social phenomenon. In the context of migrant integration, hate politics often manifests through discriminatory practices and policies. Bleich [48] notes that contemporary anti-hate policies evolved from efforts to combat racism, particularly in post-World War II Europe, addressing issues like xenophobia and racism that continue to impact migrant integration. James and McBride [45, 46] further argue that hate studies have expanded to include various forms of bias-motivated violence, highlighting ongoing challenges faced by marginalized communities in achieving social integration.

The politics of hate can manifest in numerous ways, such as online hate groups, misinformation, and ideological extremism [49–51]. These forms of hate can severely impact the social integration of migrants and refugees, leading to increased discrimination, violence, and exclusion. The rise of populist and right-wing politics has further fueled xenophobia and hate crimes against migrants. Bleich [48] notes that the term "hate" has been a mobilizing concept in the United States since the 1980s, leading to hate crime laws intended to protect marginalized groups. However, these laws also underscore the persistent presence of hate in societal structures. James and McBride [45, 46] highlight that hate studies now address the intersectionality of identities, recognizing compounded discrimination faced by individuals belonging to multiple marginalized groups. However, these laws also underscore the persistent presence of hate in societal structures. James and McBride [45, 46] highlight that hate studies now address the intersectionality of identities, recognizing compounded discrimination faced by individuals belonging to multiple marginalized groups. This complex interplay of factors underscores the need for comprehensive approaches to combat the politics of hate and promote social integration for migrants and refugees.

Despite experiencing hate speech, social exclusion, and discrimination, North Korean migrants in Seoul and New Malden are not portrayed as victims in this study. Instead, the focus is on how these migrants address these challenges and cultivate agency to peacefully confront the politics of hate as structural violence, such as social exclusion and discrimination, by developing peacebuilding capacities and adaptive strategies. The study explores the transformation of their civic identities through transnational migration from North Korea to South Korea, and the United Kingdom, and the adaptive strategies they develop to integrate successfully into their host countries. This chapter examines the dynamic nature of "bridging civic identities" among migrants and how these identities are influenced by their transnational journeys. Additionally, the research investigates the potential for migrants to contribute to social cohesion and societal change.

4. Bridging civic identities

In the context of North Korean migrants navigating the politics of hate in Seoul and New Malden, the concept of "bridging civic identity" emerges as a powerful framework for understanding their potential role in social transformation. Cheong

[18] defines "bridge citizens" as individuals within conflict-affected societies who facilitate the creation of new civic knowledge, values, norms, and identities, enabling the transformation of "conflict-attuned civic identities" into "peacebuilding civic identities." This concept is particularly relevant to North Korean migrants who, despite facing hate speech, social exclusion, and discrimination, demonstrate remarkable resilience and agency in confronting these challenges.

The "bridging civic identity" of North Korean migrants is characterized by cosmopolitanism, interconnectedness, and imaginativeness [52–55]. Their cosmopolitan outlook allows them to value human life regardless of group affiliations, fostering social justice across diverse communities. This perspective is crucial in overcoming the divisive politics of hate they encounter. The interconnected nature of their identity enables them to draw links across different contexts, cultures, and experiences, building bridging social capital [56] that facilitates more inclusive and interconnected perspectives [57]. This ability is particularly valuable in navigating the complex sociopolitical landscapes of Seoul and New Malden.

Furthermore, the imaginative aspect of their bridging civic identity allows North Korean migrants to envision a future society characterized by social justice [53, 58]. This forward-looking perspective is essential in developing peacebuilding capacities and adaptive strategies to confront structural violence and discrimination. The civic component of their identity emphasizes their capacity for agency and social change [52, 58–61].

By developing these bridging civic identities, North Korean migrants in Seoul and New Malden are not merely victims of the politics of hate, but active agents of social transformation. Their unique experiences and perspectives position them as potential catalysts for social cohesion, contributing to the peaceful transformation of conflict-attuned civic identities into peacebuilding ones. This transformation process, rooted in their transnational experiences and adaptive strategies, exemplifies how marginalized groups can become instrumental in fostering social justice and overcoming the divisive forces of hate politics.

5. Methodological core

5.1 Research design: Autobiographical narrative inquiry

This study employed an autobiographical narrative inquiry to explore the experiences of North Korean migrants in South Korea and the UK. The research design combined biographical narrative interviews and digital autobiographical writing to gain deep insights into participants' lived experiences and identity formation processes.

Seven participants (four females and three males) aged 18–40 were recruited through purposive sampling [62], representing diverse *songbun* (social classification system in North Korea) backgrounds. This sampling strategy ensured a range of perspectives from different social strata within North Korean society. The participants' backgrounds spanned from the highest "core class" to the lowest "hostile class," providing a comprehensive view of experiences across the social spectrum.

5.2 Data collection

Research about conflict-affected settings is known to be constrained by methodological challenges (see, for example, [63]) and ethical complexities (see, for example, [64–66]). In this case, I attempted to anticipate and mitigate some of these challenges in different ways, which are detailed below alongside the descriptions of the data-gathering processes.

The data from the Korean migrant youths were collected from October 2017 to February 2019. To mitigate the methodological constraint of having a small sample size, which is characteristic of conflict-related research [67, 68], the researcher used the combination of the digital autobiographical writing method and biographical narrative interviews [5, 6], which allowed for comprehensiveness, enabling the authors to intimately explore participants' life trajectories from their experiences of life in North Korea, their journeys of escape and migration, their adaptive strategies in South Korea and the UK. The interviewer's proficiency in Korean also ensured that the interviews captured and interpreted nuances and emotions, enhancing the richness of the gathered data.

In addition, data was collected through biographical narrative interviews lasting three to four hours each, conducted between 2017 and 2019 in Seoul and New Malden. Four participants also completed digital autobiographical journals over several months using Google Docs, allowing for multimodal expression through text, images, and links.

5.3 Participant profiles

The study's participants were purposefully sampled to ensure a diverse representation of North Korean migrants. The seven participants, aged between 18 and 40, included four females and three males, each with a different *songbun* status, which is a unique social classification system in North Korea. Their backgrounds ranged from the core class to the hostile class, and they had varied educational and career experiences (**Table 1**).

Participants' pseudonyms	Place of residence	*Songbun* status	Gender	Age	Profession
Geum	ROK (since 2009)	Wavering class (New entrepreneurial class)	F	31	Florist
Hyang	ROK (since 2013)	Wavering class	F	21	Student (Business Management)
Ju	ROK (since 2011)	Core class to wavering class	M	26	Student (Political science)
Kweon	ROK (since 2012)	Father: Core class mother: Hostile class	M	26	Student (Fine Art)
Hae	UK (since 2005)	Hostile class	F	25 (28)	Student (International development)
Ha-young	UK (since 2007)	Hostile class	F	40	Housewife
Min-seok	UK (since 2007)	N/A	M	19	Student (Computer science)

Note. All participants were given pseudonyms to ensure anonymity, as per the Research Ethics Committee of the Institute of Education at UCL's Code of Ethics, 2017. Some personal details have been removed to protect their identities.

Table 1.
Profile of research participants.

5.4 Data analysis

Interpretative Phenomenological Analysis (IPA) was used across a set of data. Following the five stages outlined by Smith et al. [69], I first focused on the microscopic details of the individual participants' accounts. Across multiple readings, I noted anything of interest from the data and made exploratory comments in three ways: descriptive, linguistic, and conceptual. I identified significant words, phrases, or statements in the original transcriptions while asking myself what these meant, what the participants meant, and what the participants wanted to narrate, assuming their cultural/social backgrounds and experiences. I applied an interpretation-focused coding strategy [70] to reach the essential meaning of the empirical indicator identified in the third stage of IPA. Throughout the process of identifying the indicators for making meaning, I generated emergent themes, linking them to each context, Seoul and New Malden. In Seoul, the emergent themes are categorized as follows: Division habitus-(1) Hatred based on perceived character and identity; (2) Structural and cultural violence; (3) Institutionalized Bias: The Role of Education in Normalizing Inferiority and Discrimination. In New Malden, the emerging themes are categorized as follows: Challenges Faced by North Korean Refugees in New Malden- (1) language barriers, (2) acculturation and cultural belonging, (3) legal barrier and identity conflict.

With the aid of NVIVO12, I looked for connections across the emergent ideas and searched for cross-case patterns, ensuring that the themes that were generated were present across both sets of data. This process was repeated until the themes became explicit and meaningfully covered the accounts' major results. I eventually generated two superordinate themes—(1) politics of hate and (2) being bridges—with corresponding sub-themes.

To ensure the validity and reliability of data analysis, I gathered data from multiple sources, using various strategies, including biographical narrative interviews, digital autobiographical writing, informal conversations, researcher's field notes, and reflective journals. In analyzing the North Korean migrants' data, I employed CAQDAS and member checks, using NVIVO 12.

6. Findings

6.1 Division habitus in South Korea

The concept of "division habitus" is rooted in Bourdieu's [71] theory of habitus which refers to the ingrained habits, skills, and dispositions that individuals acquire through their life experiences. In the context of the politics of hate in South Korea, division habitus emerges from the territorial and ideological division of the Korean Peninsula, shaping the civic identities of these migrants and creating a symbolic boundary between "us" (South Koreans) and "them" (North Korean migrants) [72, 73]. This boundary is reinforced by historical and ongoing conflicts, leading to exclusion and discrimination against North Korean migrants in South Korean society. The division habitus legitimizes enmity and exacerbates structural and cultural violence, making adaptation to South Korean society particularly challenging for North Korean migrants [34, 37]. This exclusion is not merely social but is deeply embedded in the political and cultural fabric of South Korean society [74–76].

In addition, the politics of hate experienced by North Korean migrants living in South Korea are complex and multifaceted, reflecting their unique dual status as both transnational migrants and citizens of a divided nation. This dual status contributes to the politics of hate in Korean society, as the division system has led to the development of different values, norms, and identities between the two Koreas over the past half-century [16, 30, 40]. Drawing on the characteristics of the politics of hate described earlier and the participants' narratives, three key aspects of this phenomenon can be examined: (1) Hatred based on perceived character and identity; (2) Structural and cultural violence; (3) Institutionalized Bias: The Role of Education in Normalizing Inferiority and Discrimination.

6.1.1 Hatred based on perceived character and identity

The politics of hate experienced by North Korean migrants often stems from South Koreans' negative perceptions of their character and identity [34]. This aligns with Aristotle's conception of hatred as a response to perceived negative qualities in others. The perception of North Korean migrants as opponents in a wider sociopolitical context leads to strict monitoring and control, as they are viewed as suspicious communists [10, 11, 77, 78]. This perception contributes to the marginalization and stigmatization of North Korean migrants due to their North Korean identity [10, 27, 79, 80], as evidenced by the experiences of migrants like Ha-young, who faced sarcasm, neglect, and discrimination. As one participant, Ju, recounts:

> "Anti-communism, [I would say as] anti-North Koreanism, and hatred are still pervasive at all levels of the South Korean society."

This statement reflects how North Korean migrants are often viewed as embodiments of an enemy ideology, rather than as individuals. The hatred directed at them is not based on personal offenses, but on their perceived identity as North Koreans. This group-based antipathy fits with the Aristotelian notion that hatred can be felt toward "types" of people.

The marginalization and stigmatization of North Korean migrants due to their North Korean identity further exacerbate the politics of hate. As previous research [10, 27, 79, 80] discusses, North Korean migrants are often stigmatized due to their background. This is evident in the experiences of Ha-young, who never used North Korean dialects at home out of fear that her children would face discrimination. Similarly, Hyang dropped out of a public school after one month, finding it hard to hide her North Korean identity as her teacher had recommended. These experiences demonstrate how the politics of hate can manifest in everyday interactions, forcing North Korean migrants to suppress their identities to avoid discrimination.

6.1.2 Structural and cultural violence

The politics of hate manifests in systemic and cultural violence against North Korean migrants, reflecting the broader societal structures that perpetuate discrimination [43, 81]. This aligns with modern conceptions of hate as embedded in social and cultural norms. For instance, Hyang noted that whenever her peers chatted using newly coined slang words, she could not understand at all, highlighting the language barrier that contributes to feelings of isolation and being seen as outsiders. This language barrier is not just a practical issue, but a form of cultural violence that isolates and alienates North Korean migrants. It represents a systemic failure to accommodate their needs and experiences, reinforcing their outsider status.

6.1.3 Institutionalized bias: The role of education in normalizing inferiority and discrimination

The politics of hate against North Korean migrants is often normalized and internalized by the formal education system in South Korea. This reflects the modern understanding of hate as often subtle and pervasive, rather than always overt.

The South Korean government has established policies and programs to support North Koreans' resettlement and education [82]. *Hanawon* provides a three-month training program covering South Korean society, career counseling, emotional support, and more. Special admission and transfer options, tuition exemptions, scholarships, and other educational benefits are available. Transition schools like *Hangyeore* help migrant youth adapt before transferring to mainstream schools [83].

However, the South Korean education system also disadvantages North Korean youth. Many are placed two to three grade levels below their age, making them feel like outsiders among younger South Korean classmates. Lack of digital literacy puts them behind their highly tech-savvy Southern peers. Kweon's observation captures this: "North Korean migrant youths were no match for Southern counterparts." This statement suggests an internalized sense of inferiority among North Korean migrants, reflecting how the politics of hate can shape self-perception and limit aspirations. The focus on criticizing North Korea in schools engendered the gap between the people of the two Koreas and reinforced the division habitus. Assimilationist policies pressure them to quickly shed their North Korean identities, which are seen as inherent deficits.

6.1.4 Becoming Jayumin citizen

Despite these challenges, the informal education system, social support networks, and personal efforts play a crucial role in helping North Korean migrants form a new civic identity, known as the "*Jayumin* identity," characterized by resilience and proactive engagement with their new environment. For example, participants like Ju, Hyang, and Kweon have taken advantage of these informal educational opportunities such as cram schools and alternative schools to achieve their academic goals.

Ju, who had no formal schooling in the North, prepared for and passed the Korean College Scholastic Aptitude Test (CSAT) in South Korea, eventually entering one of the nation's prestigious universities to study political science. Similarly, Kweon, who aspired to become a painter, received support from NGOs and Christian organizations to study fine art at a university in South Korea. Despite a series of challenges to adapt to the Korean public education system, Hyang ended up getting into one of the prestigious universities to study business management in South Korea.

Similarly, Geum's story illustrates how personal initiative combined with social support can lead to success. She studied English abroad and earned a florist diploma with NGO support in London. She now runs a thriving floral business in Seoul. This story shows how access to resources and support, combined with personal determination, can help North Korean migrants overcome barriers and establish successful lives in South Korea.

In conclusion, the politics of hate experienced by North Korean migrants in South Korea is deeply rooted in historical division, cultural differences, and societal prejudices. It manifests in various forms, from overt discrimination to subtle cultural alienation. However, the experiences of participants like Ju and Geum demonstrate that with appropriate support systems, educational opportunities, and personal resilience, it is possible for North Korean migrants to overcome these challenges. They can develop a "*Jayumin* identity" that bridges their North Korean background with their new life in South Korea, contributing positively to society and potentially playing a crucial role in future reconciliation efforts. This process of identity transformation and integration, while challenging, offers hope for overcoming the politics of hate and building a more inclusive society.

6.2 New Malden, a cosmopolitan space in the UK

Unlike South Korea, which has a relatively short history of migration, the UK has a long history of immigration, which has shaped its policies and societal attitudes toward migrants. New Malden, a suburban area in southwest London, has emerged as a unique cosmopolitan space in the United Kingdom, particularly for North Korean migrants. This multicultural enclave provides a distinctive environment where diverse communities, including North Korean refugees, South Korean immigrants, ethnic Koreans, migrants from various backgrounds, and British natives, coexist and interact. While this setting offers opportunities for intercultural exchange and the development of cosmopolitan identities, it also presents significant challenges for North Korean refugees as they navigate the complexities of integration and identity formation. North Korean migrants in the UK, in particular, face unique challenges stemming from three aspects: (1) language barriers, (2) acculturation and cultural belonging, and (3) legal barrier and identity conflict.

6.2.1 Language barriers

One of the primary hurdles faced by North Korean migrants is the language barrier. Many arrive in the UK with limited English proficiency, which impacts their ability to integrate into British society and access essential services. This linguistic challenge extends beyond basic communication to understanding cultural nuances, idioms, and slang used by native speakers. Hae and Min-seok struggled to understand slang and idioms used by their native-born peers, leading to feelings of anxiety and nervousness when communicating with friends and teachers. Hae and Min-seok, for instance, experienced anxiety and embarrassment in British schools due to their unfamiliarity with local slang and idioms, such as "wake up and smell the coffee" or "storm in a teacup." This language barrier led to feelings of marginalization and insecurity, as effective communication is crucial for interacting with native peers and teachers.

6.2.2 Acculturation and cultural belonging

The process of acculturation presents another significant challenge for North Korean refugees in New Malden. Cultural belonging also posed a major obstacle, as the migrants had to navigate a new cultural milieu with value systems that often differed from their own [84, 85]. These challenges are not unique to North Korean migrants but are part of a broader pattern of discrimination and marginalization faced by many minority groups in the UK [4, 86].

The process of acculturation can be fraught with difficulties, as migrants navigate between maintaining their cultural heritage and adapting to new societal norms [87, 88]. Hae, a North Korean refugee who has spent her adult life in the UK, reflects on this struggle: "Well, I don't think I understand 100% of each culture either. And

I don't think I can genuinely say that I am British." This sentiment highlights the profound impact of acculturation on identity formation and the sense of belonging for North Korean migrants in New Malden.

6.2.3 Legal barrier and identity conflict

Despite the UK's more inclusive policies, North Korean migrants still encounter challenges related to legal barrier and identity conflict as they move to the UK [72, 73, 89, 90]. This struggle is further complicated by the need to conceal their South Korean citizenship to secure asylum, resulting in a sense of self-denial and internal turmoil.

This self-denial of identity manifests differently among individuals. Hae, for instance, continues to live under the false identity and forged date of birth used upon entry to the UK. Even her friends remain unaware of her true identity, leading her to feel guilty about her South Korean citizenship and burdened by concealing her origins. Additionally, her experience in school illustrates the depth of this conflict. During a class discussion about a Korean War film, Hae revealed her North Korean identity, leading to a heated exchange with a South Korean-descended classmate who labeled her a "COMMIE." This incident highlights how deeply ingrained ideological tensions can resurface even in new cultural contexts. Hae's difficulty in disclosing her original nationality stems from experiences of hostility, feeling like an "enemy of the state" in South Korea and an "enemy of the world" in the UK.

Conversely, Min-seok viewed his North Korean refugee background as an advantage, believing it could garner support from advocates for minorities in British society. He saw his knowledge about North Korea as symbolic capital, potentially beneficial in his new environment. These contrasting approaches demonstrate the varied strategies North Korean migrants employ to navigate their complex identities in new societal contexts.

6.2.4 Transforming cosmopolitan civic identities

While the challenges faced by those samples in New Malden are significant, the area's unique cosmopolitan character provides opportunities for intercultural exchange and the development of more inclusive identities. The diverse composition of New Malden's population creates a rich tapestry of intercultural interactions that can foster understanding and empathy.

In New Malden, a notable Korean enclave in the UK, North Korean migrants are primarily seen as part of the broader Asian refugee community, which allows them to access social benefits and welfare systems more readily [89, 90].

New Malden's status within the broader multicultural landscape of London creates a unique environment for North Korean refugees. The diverse community in New Malden offers numerous opportunities for developing intercultural sensitivity and competence. Through daily interactions with people from various backgrounds, North Korean migrants can broaden their perspectives and develop a more nuanced understanding of cultural differences. The multilingual nature of New Malden offers unique advantages for North Korean refugees. The ability to communicate in Korean within the community while also developing English skills creates a supportive environment for language acquisition. This linguistic flexibility enhances migrants' ability to navigate between different cultural contexts and communicate effectively with various communities, including ethnic Chinese, fellow North Koreans, South Korean immigrants, and native English speakers.

The British education system played a crucial role, offering opportunities for academic growth and intercultural competence development. Hae was able to retake her General Certificate of Secondary Education (GCSE) and eventually pursue higher education, thanks to the support of her teachers and the British education policy that ensures educational equality regardless of background. Min-seok, supported by his teachers and friends, developed intercultural competencies, embracing a more inclusive worldview. The British education system, despite its challenges, provided opportunities for both Hae and Min-seok to succeed academically and socially, allowing them to navigate the complexities of their new environment.

Hae's involvement in volunteer activities with organizations like Home Office and Refugee Action exposed her to diverse backgrounds, broadening her perspective. This environment, characterized by flexible cultural and linguistic boundaries, allowed them to communicate effectively with various communities, including ethnic Chinese, fellow North Koreans, South Korean immigrants, and native English speakers. Through these interactions, Hae and Min-seok developed a cosmopolitan civic identity marked by empathy, inclusivity, and a sense of global citizenship. This perspective allows them to see beyond national identities and recognize shared human experiences across cultural boundaries. This empathetic perspective extends not only to fellow refugees but to other marginalized groups, contributing to a more inclusive society. Hae's reflection on her identity struggles illustrates the development of a nuanced, empathetic perspective: "Sometimes I feel in the middle of belonging nowhere. If I think about my identity as British, I question myself, am I deeply rooted in this country?"

Min-seok's experience illustrates this potential for growth: "Regardless of my current national identity, which is British. I wish to emphasise the fact that I am North Korean by blood because as a person whose existence results from many sacrifices that my mother and my father made; I do not wish to abandon my origins and I want to do everything in my power to represent the better future that I want North Korea to have."

This statement reflects a complex identity that embraces both British citizenship and North Korean heritage, demonstrating the potential for developing a cosmopolitan civic identity that transcends narrow national identities. Their experiences in New Malden highlight how intercultural contacts and education can contribute to resolving the politics of hate and fostering a more inclusive society.

In conclusion, the case of North Korean migrants in New Malden demonstrates how intercultural contacts and education can play a pivotal role in resolving the politics of hate. By engaging with diverse cultural groups and receiving support from the British government, these migrants were able to overcome the discrimination and marginalization they initially faced. Their experiences underscore the significance of intercultural sensitivity and empathy in building a more inclusive society and highlight the transformative power of education and supportive policies in fostering a sense of belonging and cosmopolitan civic identity.

7. Navigating politics of hate of north Korean migrants: Path to becoming bridge citizen

The politics of hate experienced by North Korean migrants in Seoul, South Korea is deeply rooted in the historical and ideological division of the Korean Peninsula, which has created a division habitus that distinguishes "us" from "them." This division habitus manifests in structural and cultural violence, where North Korean migrants face exclusion and discrimination due to their perceived identity as suspicious communists [10, 11, 78]. The marginalization is further exacerbated by the educational system, which often places North Korean youth at a disadvantage, reinforcing feelings of inferiority and alienation [74, 75, 91]. Despite these challenges, some migrants have managed to overcome these barriers through education and social support, forming a "*Jayumin* identity" that bridges their North Korean background with their new life in South Korea.

In contrast, the Politics of Hate for North Korean migrants in New Malden, the UK is thus characterized by a complex interplay of racial discrimination common to Asian migrants, specific prejudices related to North Korea's global image such as "Nuclear Armed State" and intra-community dynamics within migrant groups. This multifaceted discrimination aligns with what Anthias [92] describes as "translocational positionality," where individuals face intersecting forms of exclusion based on their various identities and social locations. For North Korean migrants, navigating this landscape requires negotiating multiple layers of identity and belonging in ways that differ significantly from their experiences in South Korea.

In addition, North Korean migrants still face specific challenges related to their national origin. They may experience what Garapich [4] terms "hierarchies of deservingness" among migrant communities, where some groups are perceived as more deserving of acceptance than others. North Koreans, coming from a politically isolated and negatively portrayed country, may find themselves low in this hierarchy. This can lead to experiences of exclusion not just from British society, but also from within Korean immigrant communities such as New Malden [72, 73]. Furthermore, the role of international organizations and civil society in combating hate crime is crucial for North Korean migrants. Cooperation between criminal justice agencies and civil society can create a more supportive environment, helping refugees navigate discrimination and build peacebuilding capacities [93, 94]. The findings from these studies underscore the importance of compassionate migration policies and the need for a multi-layered approach to address the politics of hate, ultimately fostering a more inclusive and empathetic society.

Overcoming the politics of hate requires both structural support and personal resilience. In South Korea, the government has implemented various educational policies and support systems, such as the *Hanawon* adaptation program, which includes language education, career counseling, and emotional stability modules [95]. These programs have enabled migrants like Ju and Kweon to achieve academic success and engage in civic activities, contributing positively to society. Similarly, in New Malden, the diverse community offers opportunities for intercultural exchange and the development of more inclusive identities. The ability to communicate in Korean within the community while developing English skills creates a supportive environment for language acquisition, enhancing migrants' ability to navigate between different cultural contexts.

The concept of "bridge citizens" offers a powerful framework for understanding how North Korean migrants can overcome the politics of hate and contribute to social transformation. By developing a "bridging civic identity" characterized by cosmopolitanism, interconnectedness, and imaginativeness, these migrants can help bridge the gaps between different communities and foster mutual understanding. In Seoul, this might involve helping South Koreans understand the complexities of North Korean experiences, while in New Malden, it could mean facilitating connections between various migrant communities and the broader British society.

The cosmopolitan nature of this identity, valuing every human regardless of group affiliation, aligns with the experiences of participants who have successfully navigated multiple cultural contexts. The interconnected aspect is evident in how migrants draw links across different experiences and cultures, building bridging social capital [56]. Finally, the imaginative component is reflected in the migrants' ability to envision and work toward a more inclusive future society. As North Korean migrants in both Seoul and New Malden continue to develop these bridging civic identities, they have the potential to become powerful agents of change, transforming conflict-attuned civic identities into peacebuilding ones. This transformation not only helps them overcome the politics of hate in their current contexts but also positions them as crucial bridge citizens in the potential future of a unified Korea, where their unique experiences and perspectives can contribute to building a more inclusive and peaceful society.

8. Conclusion

In conclusion, the study of North Korean migrants in Seoul and New Malden reveals the profound impact of the politics of hate on their integration and civic identity transformation. Despite facing significant discrimination and structural violence rooted in territorial divisions in the Korean peninsula, these migrants demonstrate resilience by developing a "*Jayumin* identity," which bridges their North Korean heritage with their new lives in the South. This identity transformation is supported by educational opportunities and social networks that empower them to overcome societal prejudices. In contrast, the cosmopolitan environment of New Malden offers a unique space for North Korean migrants to cultivate cosmopolitan civic identities that embrace interconnectedness and imaginativeness. They navigate challenges such as language barriers and cultural belonging while leveraging the supportive multicultural landscape to foster intercultural sensitivity and cosmopolitanism. These experiences underscore the potential of North Korean migrants to become bridge citizens—individuals who not only overcome the politics of hate but also contribute to social cohesion and peacebuilding efforts in their communities. By leveraging educational opportunities, social networks, and their unique transnational perspectives, young North Korean migrants are transforming conflict-attuned civic identities into peacebuilding ones. In this sense, this study emphasizes the importance of supportive policies for migrants and practices that recognize the transformative potential of migrants as agents of positive social change, ultimately contributing to a more inclusive and peaceful society.

Conflict of interest

The authors declare no conflict of interest.

Thanks

While conducting the research, I was deeply moved by the resilience of young North Korean migrants. Their determination to make the most of every moment has been a powerful inspiration for this study. I am incredibly grateful for their support and participation.

Author details

Stella Micheong Cheong
Yonsei University, Seoul, Republic of Korea

*Address all correspondence to: s.cheong@yonsei.ac.kr

IntechOpen

© 2024 The Author(s). Licensee IntechOpen. This chapter is distributed under the terms of the Creative Commons Attribution License (http://creativecommons.org/licenses/by/4.0), which permits unrestricted use, distribution, and reproduction in any medium, provided the original work is properly cited.

References

[1] Dickens C. A Tale of Two Cities. Chapman and Hall; 1859/1866

[2] Park SJ. The paradox of postcolonial Korean nationalism: State-sponsored cultural policy in South Korea, 1965-present. Journal of Korean Studies. 2010a;**15**(1):67-93. DOI: 10.1353/jks.2010.0002

[3] Park YG. Philosophical reflection on the habitus of division. Journal of Philosophical Thought in Korea. 2010b;**21**(3):369-411

[4] Garapich MP. London's Polish Borders: Transnationalizing Class and Ethnicity among Polish Migrants in London. Columbia University Press; 2016

[5] Schütze F. Cognitive figures of autobiographical extempore narration. In: Miller R, editor. Biographical Research Methods. London: Sage Publications; 1984. pp. 289-338), Volume II

[6] Schütze F. Biography Analysis on the Empirical Base of Autobiographical Narratives: How to Analyse Autobiographical Narrative Interviews–Part I, pp. 153-204. 2007. Available from: http://www.profit.uni.lodz.pl/pub/dok/6ca34cbaf07ece58cbd1b4f24371c8c8/European_Studies_2

[7] Cheong SMC, Azada-Palacios R, Beye K. Becoming bridge citizens: Educating for social justice in conflict-affected settings. Education, Citizenship and Social Justice. 2024. DOI: 10.1177/17461979231222904

[8] National Institute of Korean History. The History of the Republic of Korea. Seoul: National Institute of Korean History; 2002

[9] Cumings B. Korea's Place in the Sun: A Modern History. W. W. Norton and Company; 1997

[10] Kim SK. "defector, " "refugee," or "migrant"? North Korean settlers in South Korea's changing social discourse. North Korean Review. 2012a;**8**(2):94-110

[11] Kim YY. Ideology, identity, and intercultural communication: An analysis of differing academic conceptions of cultural identity. Journal of Intercultural Communication Research. 2012b;**36**(3):237-253. DOI: 10.1080/17475750701737181

[12] Emamdjomeh A, Karklis L, Meko T. This Thin Ribbon of Land Separates North and South Korea: Why Should We Care? The Washington Post [Online]. 2017. Available from: https://www.washingtonpost.com/graphics/2017/world/mapping-the-dmz/ [Accessed: February 20, 2024]

[13] Cumings B. Divided Korea: United future? Foreign Policy. 1995;**99**:123-138. DOI: 10.2307/1149008

[14] Fields KJ. The Global Transformation of Time: 1870-1950. Cambridge, MA: Harvard University Press; 2019

[15] Ford G. Talking to North Korea: Ending the Nuclear Standoff. London: Pluto Press; 2018

[16] Paik N-C. The Division System in Crisis: Essays on Contemporary Korea. EScholarship: University of California Press; 2011

[17] Paik N-C. Toward overcoming Korea's division system through civic participation. Critical Asian Studies. 2013;**45**(2):279-290

[18] Cheong MC. Imagining Peacebuilding Citizenship Education: An Investigation of the Experience of North Korean Migrants as 'Bridge Citizens' Doctoral thesis. London: University College London; 2022

[19] Heo M. The political economy of North Korea: Identities, histories, and worldviews. Journal of Asian Security and International Affairs. 2019;**6**(1):111-132. DOI: 10.1177/2347797019831228

[20] Honneth A. The Struggle for Recognition: The Moral Grammar of Social Conflicts, trans. J Anderson. Cambridge: Polity Press. 1995/1992

[21] Jung J-H. Refugee and religious narratives: The conversion of North Koreans from refugees to God's warriors. In: Horstmann A, Jung J-H editors. Building Noah's Ark for Migrants, Refugees, and Religious Communities. New York: Palgrave Macmillan US; 2015. pp. 77-100

[22] Kim SY. The politics of nationalism in U.S.-Korean relations. Journal of International and Area Studies. 2006;**13**(2):21-37

[23] Lankov A. The Real North Korea: Life and Politics in the Failed Stalinist Utopia. New York: Oxford University Press; 2014

[24] Kang JW. The "enemy" the Korean war: A self-critical retrospective. Critical Asian Studies. 2011a;**43**(3):399-421. DOI: 10.1080/14672715.2011.597338

[25] Cornell University, INSEAD, WIPO. The Global Innovation Index 2020: Who Will Finance Innovation? 2020. Available from: https://www.wipo.int/edocs/pubdocs/en/wipo_pub_gii_2020.pdf

[26] Kim KS. The Development of Modern South Korea: State Formation, Capitalist Development and National Identity. London: Routledge; 2008

[27] Kang JW. Being a Korean citizen: Disciplinary governance of Korea and differentiation of identity of settlers in NK. Korean Journal of Sociology. 2011;**45**(1):191-227

[28] Moon KHS. Protesting America: Democracy and the U.S.-Korea Alliance. Berkeley, CA: University of California Press; 2012

[29] Seth M. Education zeal, state control and citizenship in South Korea. Citizenship Studies. 2012;**16**(1):13-28. DOI: 10.1080/13621025.2012.651400

[30] Choi S. Ethnic brethren and the national "other": North Korean youths in South Korea. Oxford Monitor of Forced Migration. 2011;**1**(2):51-57

[31] Chung BH. Between defector and migrant: Identities and strategies of north Koreans in South Korea. Korean Studies. 2008;**32**(1):1-27. DOI: 10.1353/ks.0.0002

[32] Kim SK. Everyday life and cultural citizenship of north Korean settlers in South Korea. In: Kim S, Choi J, editors. The Everyday Life of North Koreans. Lanham, MD: Lexington Books; 2014. pp. 155-174

[33] Lankov A. Bitter taste of paradise: North Korean refugees in South Korea. Journal of East Asian Studies. 2006;**6**(1):105-137. DOI: 10.1017/S1598240800000059

[34] Yang MS, Lee WY, Lee HY. A study on mutual awareness of residents of North and South Korea. Unification policy studies. Seoul: Korea Institute of National Unification; 2019;**28**(1):105-133. DOI: 10.33728/ups.2019.28.1.005

[35] Galtung J. Violence, peace, and peace research. Journal of Peace Research. 1969;**6**(3):167-191. DOI: 10.1177/002234336900600301

[36] Galtung J. Three approaches to peace: Peacekeeping, peacemaking, and peacebuilding. In: Galtung J, editor. Peace, War and Defense: Essays in Peace Research. Vol. 2. Copenhagen: Christian Ejlers; 1976. pp. 282-304

[37] Galtung J. Cultural violence. Journal of Peace Research. 1990;**27**(3):291-305. DOI: 10.1177/0022343390027003005

[38] Bourdieu P. Distinction: A Social Critique of the Judgement of Taste. Harvard University Press; 1984

[39] Pavlenko A, Norton B. Imagined communities, identity, and English language learning. In: Cummins J, Davison C, editors. International Handbook of English Language Teaching. Boston, MA: Springer; 2007. pp. 669-680. DOI: 10.1007/978-0-387-46301-8_43

[40] Kim KS, Park JH. Multiculturalism and ethnic nationalism in South Korea: Focusing on the relations between the state and civil society. Asian Ethnicity. 2021;**22**(1):1-18. DOI: 10.1080/14631369.2020.1814598

[41] Aristotle. Rhetoric (Freese JH, Trans.). Cambridge, MA: Harvard University Press; 1926

[42] Brudholm T. Hatred beyond bigotry. In: Hall N, Corb A, Giannasi P, Grieve J, editors. The Oxford Handbook of Hate Crime. Oxford: Oxford University Press; 2018. pp. 53-75

[43] Perry B. In: The Name of Hate: Understanding Hate Crimes. New York: Routledge; 2001

[44] Yar M. Critical criminology, critical theory and social harm. In: Hall S, Winlow S, editors. New Directions in Criminological Theory. London: Routledge; 2012. pp. 52-65

[45] James M, McBride KD. The politics of hate: Implications for social work. Social Work. 2022a;**67**(1):5-12. DOI: 10.1093/sw/swab048

[46] James Z, McBride K. Critical hate studies: A new perspective. International Review of Victimology. 2022b;**28**(1):92-108

[47] Tsai RL. Introduction: The politics of hate. Journal of Hate Studies. 2012;**10**(1):9-13. Available from: http://journals.gonzaga.edu/index.php/johs/article/view/176

[48] Bleich E. Historical institutionalism and judicial decision-making: Ideas, institutions, and actors in French hate speech laws. World Politics. 2018;**70**(1):53-85. DOI: 10.1017/S0043887117000193

[49] Chau M, Xu J. The impact of social media on political participation. Journal of Political Science. 2007;**35**(2):251-265

[50] Engesser S, Ernst N, Esser F, Büchel F. Populism and social media: How politicians spread a fragmented ideology. Information, Communication and Society. 2017;**20**(8):1109-1126. DOI: 10.1080/1369118X.2016.1207697

[51] Ogbuoshi LI, Eze CC, Kuma-Abang M. Hate speech and social media: A critical discourse analysis of selected Facebook posts. Journal of Literature, Languages and Linguistics. 2019;**54**:1-10

[52] Appiah KA. Cosmopolitanism: Ethics in a World of Strangers. New York: W. W. Norton and Company; 2007

[53] Kanno Y, Norton B. Imagined communities and educational possibilities: Introduction. Journal of Language, Identity and Education. 2003;**2**(4):241-249. DOI: 10.1207/S15327701JLIE0204_1

[54] Nussbaum M. Upheavals of Thought: The Intelligence of Emotions. Cambridge, England: Cambridge University Press; 2001

[55] Osler A, Starkey H. Changing Citizenship: Democracy and Inclusion in Education. Maidenhead, UK: Open University Press; 2005

[56] Putnam RD. Bowling Alone: The Collapse and Revival of American Community. New York: Simon and Schuster; 2000

[57] Zuckerman E. Rewire: Digital Cosmopolitans in the Age of Connection. New York, NY: WW Norton; 2013

[58] Norton B. Identity and Language Learning: Extending the Conversation. 2nd ed. Bristol, UK: Multilingual Matters; 2013

[59] Beck U. Mobility and the cosmopolitan perspective. In: Canzler W, Kaufmann V, Kesselring S, editors. Tracing Mobilities: Towards a Cosmopolitan Perspective. Farnham, UK: Ashgate Publishing; 2008. pp. 25-35

[60] Reardon BA. Meditating on the barricades: Concerns, cautions, and possibilities for peace education for political efficacy. In: Trifonas PP, Wright B, editors. Critical Peace Education: Difficult Dialogues. Dordrecht; London: Springer; 2012. pp. 1-28

[61] Starkey H. Learning to live together: Children's rights, identities and citizenship. In: Edge K, editor. Transnational Perspectives on Democracy, Citizenship, Human Rights and Peace Education. London: Bloomsbury Academic; 2019. pp. 179-196. DOI: 10.5040/9781350052369.ch-009

[62] Ims KJ, Pedersen LJT, Zsolnai L. Qualitative research in business ethics. Journal of Business Ethics. 2021;**171**(1):1-4. DOI: 10.1007/s10551-021-04848-7

[63] Cohen N, Arieli T. Field research in conflict environments: Methodological challenges and snowball sampling. Journal of Peace Research. 2011;**48**(4):423-435. DOI: 10.1177/0022343311405698

[64] Campbell SP. Ethics of research in conflict environments. Journal of Global Security Studies. 2017;**2**(1):89-101. DOI: 10.1093/jogss/ogw024

[65] Kostovicova D, Knott E. Harm, change and unpredictability: The ethics of interviews in conflict research. Qualitative Research. 2022;**22**(1):56-73. DOI: 10.1177/1468794120975657

[66] Zwi AB, Grove NJ, Mackenzie C, Pittaway E, Zion D, Silove D, et al. Placing ethics in the Centre: Negotiating new spaces for ethical research in conflict situations. Global Public Health. 2006;**1**(3):264-267

[67] Clark JA. Field research methods in the Middle East. PS. Political Science and Politics. 2006;**39**(3):417-424. DOI: 10.1017/S1049096506060707

[68] Romano D. Conducting research in the Middle East's conflict zones. Political Science and Politics. 2006;**39**(03):439-441

[69] Smith JA, Flowers P, Larkin M. Interpretative Phenomenological Analysis: Theory, Method and Research. Los Angeles: Sage Publications; 2009

[70] Adu P. A Step-by-Step Guide to Qualitative Data Coding. London: Routledge; 2019

[71] Bourdieu P. The Logic of Practice. Stanford, CA: Stanford University Press; 1990

[72] Lee S. North Korean defectors in South Korea: Arduous escape and difficult integration. Asian Journal of Peacebuilding. 2019a;7(2):283-304. DOI: 10.18588/201911.00a063

[73] Lee SJ. A relational understanding of 'senses of well-being' of North Korean immigrants in the U.K. Modern North Korean studies. 2019b;22(2):8-46

[74] Kim DJ. Building relationships across the boundaries: The peacebuilding role of civil society in the Korean peninsula. International Peacekeeping. 2017a;24(4):515-537. DOI: 10.1080/13533312.2017

[75] Kim YY. Integrative communication theory of cross-cultural adaptation: Intercultural Communication Core Theories, Issues, and Concepts. In: Kim YY, editor. The international Encyclopedia of Intercultural Communication. Wiley Online Library. 2017. pp. 1-12. DOI: 10.1002/9781118783665.ieicc0041

[76] Son SA. Identity, security and the nation: Understanding the South Korean response to North Korean defectors. Asian Ethnicity. 2016;17(2):171-184

[77] Ham SJ. Educating Intimate Strangers: South Korean Schooling for the North Korean Migrant Youth Paper Presented at the Annual Meeting of the 57th Annual Conference of the Comparative and International Education Society. New Orleans, LA: Hilton Riverside Hotel; 2013

[78] Kang JW. The disciplinary politics of antagonistic nationalism in militarized South and North Korea. Positions: Asia Critique. 2012;20(1):195-228. DOI: 10.1215/10679847-1471466

[79] Kang JW. The Unending Korean War: Sovereignty, Memory, and the Politics of Division. Durham, NC: Duke University Press; 2020

[80] Kim DC. Changes in north Korean refugees' identity during their adaptation process in South Korea: A grounded theory study. Korean Journal of Social Welfare. 2009;61(2):189-213

[81] Kasnitz P, Mollenkopf JH, Waters MC, Holdaway J. Inheriting the City: The Children of Immigrants Come of Age. New York: Russell Sage Foundation; 2008

[82] The Ministry of Unification (MoU). Support for North Korean Defectors. 2006. Available from: https://www.unikorea.go.kr/eng_unikorea/relations/statistics/defectors/

[83] The Ministry of Education (MoE). Education for North Korean Migrant Students. 2019. Available from: https://www.moe.go.kr/boardCnts/view.do?boardID=316\&boardSeq=79256\&lev=0\&searchType=null\&statusYN=W\&page=1\&s=moe\&m=0302\&opType=N

[84] Ellis BH. Mental health of Somali adolescent refugees: The role of trauma, stress, and perceived discrimination. Journal of Consulting and Clinical Psychology. 2010;76(2):184-193. DOI: 10.1037/0022-006X.76.2.184

[85] Farver JAM, Narang SK, Bhadha BR. East meets west: Ethnic identity, acculturation, and conflict in Asian Indian families. Journal of Family Psychology. 2002;16(3):338-350. DOI: 10.1037/0893-3200.16.3.338

[86] Bloch A. Reflections and directions for research in refugee studies. Ethnic and Racial Studies. 2020;43(3):436-459. DOI: 10.1080/01419870.2020.1677928

[87] Phillimore J. Refugees, acculturation strategies, stress and integration. Journal

of Social Policy. 2011;**40**(3):575-593. DOI: 10.1017/S0047279410000929

[88] Waldinger R. The cross-border connection: A rejoinder. Ethnic and Racial Studies. 2015;**38**(13):2305-2313

[89] Song JJ, Bell M. North Korean secondary asylum in the UK. Migration Studies. 2019;**7**(2):160-179

[90] Jung K, Dalton B, Willis J. The onward migration of north Korean refugees to Australia: In search of cosmopolitan habitus. Cosmopolitan Civil Societies. 2017;**9**(3):1-20. DOI: 10.5130/ccs.v9i3.5506

[91] Son SA. Unity, division and ideational security on the Korean peninsula: Challenges to overcoming the Korean conflict. North Korean Review. 2015:45-62

[92] Anthias F. Thinking through the lens of translocational positionality: An intersectionality frame for understanding identity and belonging. Translocations: Migration and Social Change. 2008;**4**(1):5-20

[93] Junuzovic A. Combating hate crimes: Bridging the gap between international obligations and national realities. Intersections: East European Journal of Society and Politics. 2019;**5**(4):121-139. DOI: 10.17356/ieejsp.v5i4.569

[94] Whine M. Cooperation between criminal justice agencies and civil society in combating hate crime. Crime, Law and Social Change. 2019;**71**(3):275-289

[95] The Ministry of Unification. The Unification White Paper 2019. Republic of Korea: Ministry of Unification. 2019

Chapter 6

Perspective Chapter: The Illusion of Dystopian Justice as a Means toward Social Justice. K-drama's Global Success Unveiled

Mara Santi

Abstract

Elaborating on the representation of social hardship and the struggle of the powerless in neoliberal democracies, this study focuses on the case study of four Korean TV series (The Devil Judge, Vincenzo, Again My Life, and Reborn Rich) within the context of Korean history, local TV traditions (K-dramas), and the contemporary global influence of Korean culture (K-wave). The first aim of the study is to explain how K-dramas have established themselves as a transnational phenomenon by exploring issues of cross-cutting global relevance. Secondly, the study explains how K-dramas deliver narratives about contemporary social unease and unrest caused by democratic systems proving unable to guarantee social equity. In particular, K-dramas focus on citizens investing their hopes in justice. Yet, justice is conceived as a means to achieve social equality and is therefore forced outside of the judiciary realm and entrusted with political aims. Moreover, this justice is inherently dystopian since it is achieved with unlawful or morally unacceptable means. In the end, K-dramas warn against the threats of this pursuit, which turn out to be socially harmful and fail to achieve their goals.

Keywords: South Korea, K-wave, K-drama, TV series, neoliberal society, social criticism, narratives as societal criticism, justice

1. Introduction

This study analyzes four South Korean (hereafter Korean) TV series that depict the dark side of neoliberal society and revolve around characters fighting against the injustices it brings. These characters are either antiheroes or heroes whose actions are ethically or legally disputable. Notably, these narratives convey an ambiguous message: justice seems to be delivered, but it is either dystopian or wrongfully achieved. Either way, justice is carried out outside or against the norms, dynamics, and institutions of the democratic system. These series address contemporary societal challenges in Korea, yet they engage an audience far beyond the nation's borders by tackling global issues. My goal is to discuss the messages delivered to the international viewers.

Before that, I illustrate how Korean narratives reach the global market and why they resonate with their audience. To make my point, I start with a presentation of recent Korean history, which is a digest of global phenomena compressed into a narrow time frame. This helps explain how a Korea-based representation of society can trigger self-referencing in a global audience, even though this audience is largely unaware of the nation's past and present. I then place Korean TV series (K-dramas) in the larger context of the Korean Wave (K-wave), which is the increasing international consumption of Korean cultural products. I touch upon both the evolution of the global cultural content market and the interpretative-cognitive mechanisms that allow audiences to appreciate narratives stemming from another culture. Finally, I analyze *The devil judge* (TDJ) [1], *Vincenzo* (V) [2], and *Again my life* (AML) [3] and use *Reborn rich* (RR) [4] to comment on overarching topics.

2. Korean history of the XX century

In a little over a century, Korea experienced what most of the country in the world went through over a much longer time span: colonization, civil war, division, authoritarian and dictatorial regimes, class conflicts, widening social gaps, repression of pro-democratic movements, democratization, poverty, land reform, industrialization, economic growth, affluence, compressed development, the developmental state, financial crisis, and neoliberal turn [5–9]. Korea's current status among the world's highest-income countries must be viewed against the backdrop of these upheavals, all of which left deep scars. Korea is an emblematic case as it embodies experiences of both the Global South and the Global North, which influence the country's cultural representation of contemporaneity.

From 1910 to 1945, Korea underwent Japanese colonization, which dethroned the Joseon Dynasty and pulled the country out of its stable history, forcing it into modernization. The endured sufferings, including forced labor and sexual slavery, still fuel grievances. The freed peninsula was then devastated by a civil war that began in 1950 and was halted in 1953 by a truce followed by no peace treaty. As a result, armed, diplomatic, and symbolic hostilities continue. The war left the peninsula divided, with the South in despair. The conflict also served as a battlefield for the Cold War, with the South under the tight grip of the US and the North becoming a communist dictatorship.

Postwar Korea saw slow recovery, hindered by the authoritarian regime of its first president (1948–1960) and dependency on US economic support and protection. In 1960, massive protests by students and laborers led to free elections and the establishment of a new government, which lasted until a military coup in 1961 brought Park Chung-hee to power. A very controversial figure, Park is recognized for lifting Korea out of poverty and leading an economic miracle but is blamed for his authoritarian-dictatorial leadership and for the downsides of his policy, such as extreme labor exploitation, gender inequality, and corruption. Park reshaped society, too, creating a "cast" division between an elite of ultra-wealthy families (chaebols), who gained control of the country's main resources and power, and the rest of the population. These chaebols, initially industrial enterprises (now highly diversified family-controlled conglomerates) selected and shielded by the state, acted as driving forces of the national economy and have dominated it, for better or for worse, since the onset of industrialization [10]. After Park's assassination in 1979, dictatorship went on, and so did dissent. Protests, strikes, and demonstrations intensified, leading to brutal crackdowns by the military and the police, as in the Gwangju uprising in 1980. Despite the social crisis and lack of freedom, economic growth did not slow down. Urbanization and modernization speeded up, especially in Seoul, that bid to host the Olympics of 1988 and won (1981). With the world's eyes on the country, the regime, weaker than ever, lost US support, and in 1987, Korea embraced full democracy.

In post dictatorial Korea, with the country still operating under a developmental state system, economy and society continued to progress, with GDP per capita soaring to over $10,000 in the mid-1990s (from less than $100 in the 1960s). However, exhilaration turned to despair in 1997. One year after Korea entered the Organization for Economic Cooperation and Development (OECD), the Asian financial crisis brought the country to the brink of bankruptcy. Korea saved itself through unprecedented collective suffering, efforts, and international loans. Yet, the crisis exposed the structural economic and social weaknesses and corruption problems, disguised behind as well as caused by the steady growth. Post-1998, chaebols frequently resorted to massive layoffs, plant closures, and irregular employment while increasing their political influence. Moreover, the International Monetary Fund (IMF) bailout package imposed stringent conditions of austerity, open market policies, privatization, corporate restructuring, and reduced state intervention. Although Korea never fully complied with the neoliberal orthodoxy [8], Koreans were nonetheless thrust into the neoliberal era, willingly or not.

2.1 Contemporary Korea

Having overcome the crisis, Korea emerged as a prominent global player, becoming a founding member of the G20 and a full-fledged economic power. It also climbed the Global Soft Power Index, positioning 15th in 2024 and 6th in "Education and Science" [11]. The latter achievement is unsurprising, given consistent government investments in education since the early postwar period. Education contributed to democratization, improved labor quality, and upward social mobility. This led to widespread trust in meritocracy, with education seen as a crucial social elevator. However, nowadays good education means costly expenses, enormous pressure on students due to long study hours and intense competition, and the legitimate fear that the results may not be commensurate with the efforts because of rising youth unemployment. Discouragement and dissatisfaction toward society and its institutions are growing among new generations who, with the economy slowing down for the first time in decades, do not have prospects of intergenerational upwards mobility. As a result, class divide seems ossified, more than ever.

Korea has also changed culturally. With reference to Hofstede's cultural dimensions theory [12], Korea scores 58 (on 100) on individualism [13], up from a previous rating of 18. In recent years, many countries have seen an increase in the same dimension, which is a distinctive feature of contemporary society on the global scale. Yet, Korean spike reflects a widening generational shift, whereby the new generations are markedly more individualistic. Individualism has been embedded in the narrative of meritocracy, but in reality, this is a further symptom of disaggregating social cohesion, leading to feelings of exclusion and social resentment. Social exclusion, impossible upward mobility, and the risk of downward mobility increasingly affect traditionally oppressed demographics (precarious workers, women, the elderly), already left behind by frantic growth and tumultuous history. The glass-ceiling index, measuring inequality preventing women from rising to higher socio-economic levels, consistently ranks Korea lowest among OECD countries [14]. Korea also has the highest suicide rate in the OECD, increasing over the past two decades, with economic factors affecting the elderly and competitive, success-oriented society impacting teens and young adults [15, 16].

Research shows that intergenerational upward mobility fosters democratic support, weakened by the opposite experience, especially by the middle class; moreover, public opinion tends to blame the government and state institutions when experiencing a reduction of wealth and declining welfare [17, 18]. As for Korea, scholars note that no Korean president has "left office with much credit to his[/her] name" ([19], p. 41). Yet, distrust toward the state has become even more harmful, as the declining role of the state in neoliberal societies is further diminishing citizen's hope in the democratic system. Korean public opinion also blames chaebols for exploitative and corrupting powers and their unlawful meddling with political and judicial power. People's perception of chaebols has shifted from paragons of Korea's economic miracle to national threats [10]. A peak of distrust as well as of hope for change was manifested during the Candlelight protests (2016–2017). "South Korea just showed us how to do Democracy," titled the Washington Post (cit. in [20]) when, outraged by then President Park Geun-hye's irregularities, 17 million people participated in peaceful rallies that lasted almost 6 months and took place every Saturday in Seoul's Gwanghwamun Square and in the country's major cities. The protests led to the president's impeachment and arrest and to new elections, but more importantly, it gave voice to popular frustration for soaring economic inequality and impoverished national democracy [20].

Korean popular memory is so densely stratified that it makes it possible for a Seoul's citizen to feel closeness with a US citizen blaming their government's "Winner-Take-All" policies, which turned down the middle class and allowed power to be hijacked by the superrich [21]. At the same time, Korean protectionist attitudes [22] resonate with the Arab-Muslim world's view of globalization as Western cultural imperialism and a threat to local identities [23]. That said, no matter how much potential a culture has to speak to others, it still needs a narrative and a channel to reach audiences beyond its borders. The following sections explain how the K-wave achieved this.

3. The Korean wave

First sparked in the late 1990s by the success of romantic K-dramas on the Chinese market, where it was labeled Hallyu, the K-wave spread in the early 2000s through East and South Asia and, within a decade, flowed into the Middle East, Latin and North America, Africa, and Europe [24–32]. Today, the K-wave encompasses an ever-growing attention for Korean cultural products and supports a proportional market growth in the cultural sector, which accounted for the nation's 13th export category and the largest non-manufacturing business in 2019 [33]. The wave has also led to economic side effects, such as a tourist influx multiplying from less than 5 million in 2003 to over 17.5 million visitors in 2019 [5]. I refer to pre COVID-19 data for they are not affected by the pandemic and its aftermaths. However, although the pandemic downsized production and mobility, it increased online cultural distribution and consumption, that is to say the main environment where the K-wave was already pursuing its trans-continental goal. Hence, if anything, the pandemic further raised the tide.

Today, Korea is the origin of Asia's leading transnational pop culture flow, challenging the US/UK-dominated market [34] and representing the major non-Western export of cultural products to both the Global North and South [35]. This emerging prominence in the global cultural market, along with the country's exports in other sectors (e.g., electronics), had the non-secondary side effect of repositioning Korea internationally [36], with Korean pop culture now recognized "as a cultural brand" [37, 38]. The K-wave and its national branding result from several factors, including state and industrial policies. When Korea intensified neoliberal economic policies after 1997, the national media landscape evolved from a state-directed and protected industry to a free market. Attracting capital and exporting products became essential for a small country aiming to compete internationally, leading production companies and policymakers to develop strategies for entering the international market. Korea established partnerships first with closer actors (e.g., China) and then opened up to Western-based global players [39].

3.1 The K-wave goes over-the-top

The present-day Korean content industry's penetration into the global market primarily occurs through Netflix, the leading over-the-top (OTT) streaming platform, resulting in Korea receiving the largest number of the platform's foreign co-commissions [40]. Netflix holds the largest market share globally, with 277.65 million paid memberships reported for the 2nd quarter of 2024 [41] confirming its dominant position among competitors [42] and social media too in producing and distributing cultural content. Key factors for this success include the platform's reach, variety of content, and aggressive marketing. Moreover, Netflix capitalizes its position by blurring national boundaries not only with dubbing and subtitles but also through a hyper segmentation of the genre's categories [43] and the platform's recommendation and search algorithm. The latter does not tether the audience to its nation but segments it on taste, loosening local ties and hence enhancing the transnationality of the cultural flow [44].

Since 2013, when on-demand streaming became Netflix's primary revenue generator, the platform has invested in original content to differentiate itself from traditional and cable TV broadcasting. In 2014, it commissioned its first international original series, 3% from Brazil, which became a massive success with more than 50% of its viewing hours coming from the global market [45]. 3% is a dystopian thriller that represents a competition among the non-have to get a ticket to the elitist world of the have—which is basically the same topic of Netflix's Korean best seller *Squid Game* (2021). Netflix's internationally produced originals target the cultural sensitivities of non-Western audiences and promote multiculturalism and localization to appeal to a growing global audience. As a result, non-English shows and movies now make up nearly a third of the platform's viewing, with Korean content accounting for the most-watched (9% in 2023 [46]). According to Ref. [44], the trust built by the service—the Netflix Original effect—encourages more viewers to watch Korean content marked as Netflix Originals, even if they are not Netflix's originals in a narrow sense but licensed Korean content branded as such. In short, while Netflix is riding the K-wave, the Korean industry has found a breakthrough on the world's leading OTT platform, which pushes content forward to new audiences, yielding beneficial returns on other streaming and distribution services as well as social media.

Concerns have been raised about the cultural authenticity of K-products targeting international audiences, as they incorporate global or Western themes and esthetics to appeal to foreign viewers [47, 48]. Rather than downplaying their authenticity, K-dramas and films foreground Korean's experience with global issues, concerns, and tensions. By doing this, they align themselves with global flows, and the world takes notice. It should also be noted that K-dramas that perform well in the local market are more likely to be exported and reach a foreign audience. Thus, local audience approval screens the content and pushes it beyond the country's borders. Dramas that rank high both nationally and internationally resonate with both local and global viewers, primarily through the shared experience of contemporary society and its issues. Furthermore, many contemporary series are adaptations of locally successful webtoons, such as *The Kingdom*, the first series produced by Netflix through Korean creators [45]. *The Kingdom* belongs to the (flourishing) genre of zombie-narratives, which explore social anxiety through the lens of apocalyptic contagion.

On an opposite side of the debate, the K-wave has been welcomed as a counter-flow in cultural circulation, opposing the dominance of Western products. It is probably too early or optimistic to celebrate the K-wave as a counter-hegemonic culture. The US-Western dominance is not waning, despite an anti-hegemonic and anti-Western narrative slowly but surely emerging, also within the K-wave. It is true that US-based OTT platforms are boosting the market for transnational audiovisual products, extending their reach beyond the narrow niches of initial fandoms. As an example, in 2023, more than 60% of all Netflix's members watched Korean titles [49]. However, the emergence of local markets as content producers is reinforcing US centrality in content distribution, as local markets still rely on the production capacity and distribution structures of the major global players. Consequently, one must go through Western monopolists to move from the local to the global market, where OTT platforms perform a selection and a mediation role. In this context, how did K-dramas make inroads in the global public preferences? How did the Korean industry connect with foreign markets?

3.2 The role of K-dramas

The wave began with romantic dramas, which have historically dominated the K-drama industry. However, only a minority of the most internationally watched K-dramas are purely romantic. They rather address the malaise of the neoliberal society and issues such as social and gender inequalities, injustice, power imbalances, unemployment, and class strife. Additionally, K-dramas are said to express young people's oppression and their distrust toward institutions [50]. Jin argues that the K-wave thrives because it consistently delivers politicized cultural contents [51]. As a matter of fact, K-dramas have historically incorporated social critique, particularly in romantic stories, which have always allowed for extensive social commentary through the melodramatic mode. The melodramatic mode has been embedded in K-drama's roots since the early 1920s, when it was used in stage drama and early cinema as "a popular mechanism for making sense of the unprecedented changes brought by modernity" ([52], p. 154 [53, 54]). From the representation of violent modernization under colonial rule, the melodramatic mode permeated television drama under dictatorship, continually highlighting societal ethical demands amid historical changes through tear-jerking stories revolving around families and their moral values. Manichean stories of conflicts between the socially strong and the socially weak mirrored the surging capitalistic class polarization and the daily struggle of the lower classes [52]. Class polarization has become, more than ever, a cross-genre theme in a society where wealth is inherited, poverty is passed on to the next generation, and classes "live in the same time, under the same sky, but in different worlds," like "in a faraway orbit" [4 ep. 14]. Recent studies show that K-dramas' melodramatic depiction of recurring themes, including failing justice, social inequality, and impossible class mobility, still helps viewers cope with social uncertainty and the erosion of economic democracy under neoliberal governance [52, 55].

K-drama maintained a leading position after Korean television was no longer controlled by the state and with the introduction of commercial and cable TV channels such as SBS (1991), OCN (1995), tvN (2006), and JTBC (2011). The last two decades have seen impressive growth in the quality and quantity of Korean audiovisual production, driven by competition among new market players. During this period, K-drama became the flagship product of the K-wave, coinciding with the rise of the neoliberal era. Therefore, the rise of neoliberalism aligns with the evolution of the Korean audiovisual industry. As the country grappled with the effects of late modernization and the emerging new modernity, the most pressing topics for debate led to an even more open social analysis in TV programs and films [56]. Romantic K-dramas, with their melodramatic mode, paved the way for non-romantic social criticism and introduced social critique into new transnational products. These products often delve into dystopian imaginations and explore global themes such as corruption, rampant abuse by the powerful over the powerless, the disappearance of public safety net, abuse of public power, and the loss of hope of the younger generations [57]. In a nutshell, romantic K-dramas, with their melodramatic mode, infused their inherent social critique into new and successful transnational products that break away from romantic storylines. While traditional values, family ties, and love remain prominent themes, "edgier K-dramas" featuring innovative characters and plots emerged [43], leading to a "quiet revolution" in the realm of K-dramas ([58], p. 21).

Regarding the role of OTT platforms, an analysis of the frequency and distribution of adjective keywords used by Netflix to profile its contents reveals that for Korean contents "'Dark' ranked first with 20.0%, followed by 'Suspenseful' (17.5%), 'Exciting' (15.0%), and 'Romantic' (12.5%)" ([43], p. 7030). The algorithm may suggest Korean content if you search for "Fight the system" as well. This shows how OTT platforms help to shape a new K-drama identity that diverges from the stereotypes of the romantic genre while still adhering to the melodramatic mode. As [59] argues, the resurgent success of melodramatic narratives (at least in the US) is a symptom of the public's distress over systemic exploitation and inequality, which is what K-dramas tend to thematize. This trend is also evident outside of OTT platforms, such as on social networks for content rating and forum discussions like Reddit, where viewers seek K-dramas that offer "serious and well thought out social commentary," "dramas about wealth, politics/corporate and intense conflicts," "some political or business related dramas," "K-Drama that has Game of Thrones politics centric vibes," and above all "satisfying revenge-driven dramas." The increased visibility of Korean content has also attracted male viewers, hence "dispelling the bias that Korean dramas are romance enjoyed by young female fans" ([44], p. 6963). In other words, OTT platforms and social networks are broadening the perception of K-dramas beyond the romantic and gynocentric genre. What is certain is that the global audience is responding *en masse* to K-dramas, proving that supply is meeting demand.

4. The viewers' response

Scholars attributed the first outflow of Korean content to Asia to cultural proximity, suggesting that cultures share content due to linguistic, geographical, religious, ethnic, or historical closeness. However, this perspective has been surpassed, as it does not explain K-wave's further spread to less-familiar audiences. Jin shifts the discourse from cultural proximity to transnational proximity, which implies closeness among those who share analogous issues embedded in contemporary capitalist society. Unlike hybridity, where encountering the other implies a mediation and a loss of distinctiveness, transnational proximity emphasizes the preservation of local identity in the intercultural exchanges as an alternative to Western-driven hybridity and homogenization [45, 60].

It can be assumed that TV series, compared to films and other content, enhance transnational proximity because they offer a prolonged immersive experience to viewers. On the one hand, this allows screenwriters to develop more complex narratives, resulting in more in-depth topic analysis. On the other hand, viewers can develop a deeper and more sustained connection to the story, increasing the potential for personal reflection and drawing parallels with their own lives [61]. It is therefore assumed that complex TV series can increase viewers' non-superficial commitment on both intellectual and emotional levels. Moreover, TV-series can better bridge distant cultures because viewers have more time and opportunities to develop processes crucial for understanding and empathizing with the narrative and to process the otherness they are presented with. If the viewer cannot relate to the narrative–meaning they cannot understand it or develop any degree of identification–the narrative will be a commercial flop. K-drama narratives, for a fact, succeed in relating with their target audience.

The first step in relating to a narrative involves activating top-down processing. In top-down processing, higher-level cognitive abilities, such as knowledge, expectations, and experiences, influence how the audience understands and interprets the story [62, 63]. In other words, the audience is guided by what they already know: the frameworks and mental structures stored in their memory. This allows them to organize the novelty of a story and form expectations about the narrative. Top-down processing is triggered by contextual clues from the narrative and does not necessarily rely on accurate knowledge about the fictional world or on the real world that inspires it. In the reception of K-dramas, top-down processing likely relies on limited pre-existing information, as the average global audience knows very little about Korean history and society. Paradoxically, this unfamiliarity enhances the reception of K-dramas, as the audience fills in the gaps and localizes the Korean otherness. In this process, Korean-specific traits and facts are universalized. Where the top-down processing is insufficient to delve deeper into the story, bottom-up processing begins. In the bottom-up processing, information obtained from the story itself is separated from the viewers' pre-acquired knowledge or expertise. The longer bottom-up processing lasts, the more stereotypes give way to new information, allowing the audience to better understand a new message.

Yet, for entertainment to exist, during processing, a fundamental need must be satisfied: "the need to come into contact with or relate to media characters" ([64], p. 347). For this to happen, the perception of reality is crucial. Simply put, we see the story world through the characters, and studies in brains sciences [65] and theory-of-mind prove that we approach narratives in a character-centered way, which means by focusing on the mental states of the characters, particularly the protagonist, which must be perceived as realistic by the viewer. Realizing a similarity with the characters is decisive for the audience. When looking for similarities, the audience conceive characters as real people confronted with real-life situations. If either the character or the life-situation is perceived as unreal, the narrative will be unrelatable. This similarity is triggered by an assessment of realism, which is perceived in terms of psychological and emotional plausibility even in the most unrealistic storylines such as a zombie apocalypse. Above all, similarity is assessed on the character moral plausibility [66]. Similarity, in turn, increases the likelihood of identification; therefore, plausibility is a strong predictor of identification and crucial to stimulate the audience's emotional involvement ([67], p. 843). Identification is the highest mode of narrative reception, where the audience steps out of the self-projection and internalizes the characters' point of view. Not all viewers achieve this stage of identification, which prompts the greatest enjoyment and enhances the narrative's affective impact. However, all the viewers who appreciate a narrative pass through the previous stages. Now, I'll present a few examples of what the K-drama's global audience has processed and appreciated.

5. The devil judge's dystopian justice

An example of the processes described above is TDJ's opening sequence. In a dystopian Korea, the President delivers a speech introducing the "Live Court Show" as the first step toward a "judicial reform" aimed at "restoring law and order" and "making Korea great again." The nation is experiencing a crisis, where, according to the President, "ungrounded propaganda against the privileged" has led to widespread unrest: "arson, terrorism, and ultimately the Gwanghwamun riot" [1 ep. 1]. As the President speaks, the montage alternates between scenes of social unrest, violence, and police repression, visually translating his words into the citizens' lived reality. When the President mentions the Gwanghwamun riot, only a minority of viewers are aware of the historical significance of this area in Seoul, which faces the Joseon Dynasty's Royal Palace, was once home to the now-demolished Japanese government building, now houses institution buildings, and was the epicenter of the Candlelight Protests. However, the lack of historical depth in the audience's understanding does not diminish the effectiveness or relatability of the representation. The fictional nightmarish scenario is reminiscent of similar events that have been seen and are still a reality worldwide. This grounds the show's global "commensurability" [57] in the potential realism of shared experiences of daily struggles, social conflicts, and criticism of state institutions.

A further crucial element of this depiction is the representation of class divide. The wealthy elite is shown as a few individuals in the bright, comfortable setting of the "Live Court Show" launch party, while the common people are portrayed as a mass in a dark, degraded urban exterior marked by brutality. This Manichean framing continues throughout the series only in the depiction of characters' moral traits, adhering to the tradition of the melodramatic mode that stirs indignation over injustice perpetrated by the powerful with repeated, blatant examples. However, in the subsequent episodes, society is depicted akin to any other typical advanced contemporary society, exhibiting very few conventional dystopian traits. As a matter of fact, TDJ's hypothetical Korea is a very mild dystopia or no typical dystopia at all. Typical dystopian narratives represent hellish worlds: alternative realities characterized by dysfunctional, oppressive, often post-apocalyptic societies. There is little of this in TDJ's Korea, which is facing a pandemic, financial-economic crisis, riots, abuses by the powerful, irregular militias, and the presence of an oligarchy controlling state powers, including the police, judiciary, and media. The oligarchy is disguised behind a "charitable foundation" designed to further enrich them and led by a self-proclaimed spiritual guide who is, in fact, a rapist and corrupt. There is little fiction about this world that seems much closer to the world's daily news than to a dystopian fiction. This fictional Korea faces real challenges of hundreds of countries worldwide. Moreover, in TDJ, democratic institutions are all still in place. The oligarchs fight to maintain their power and fear above all public opinion and elections that could dethrone them. Hence, on the one hand, the dystopian claim does not place TDJ in an alternative reality but highlights the setting and the story's universality beyond the specifics of the Korean context. On the other hand, this realistic depiction of a dystopian society suggests that our world may already be a dystopia. At the same time, like a true dystopian narrative, TDJ mirrors public anxieties of our time, featuring the loss of individual agency and its negative consequences on societal structures.

The true dystopia in TDJ lies in the plan orchestrated by the protagonist, the devil judge himself. After infiltrating the oligarchy, the judge convinces them to create a trial, presided over by himself, called the "Live Court Show." This show broadcasts trials live, allowing the public to vote on the defendant's guilt or innocence. The judge then makes his ruling "based on the number of votes by the audience" [1 ep. 1]. This uncommon trial addresses real-world legal themes related to both the judicial system and its perception by citizens. It focuses on criminal law as an expression of repressive power, which is to say the power used by the state to maintain order through coercion and punitive measures. The screenwriter, a former judge, adeptly uses criminal law to discuss justice and the perception of repressive right in contemporary society, proving how the Korean debate may be relevant to contemporary questions in law and society studies [68]. Criminal cases are also the most represented legal topics in narratives, for criminal offenses are where the public most often invokes the concept of justice, raising the issue of the difference between court-administered justice (a technical-procedural matter) and the justice sought by citizens, which involves moral-cultural values and the perceived proportionality between punishment and the crime's severity.

The issue posed by spectator's participation in sentencing touches on foundational legal theories and principles, such as the distinction between the right of the accused to be judged by peers and the right to be judged by independent professionals under the principle of the separation of powers. The series' judge operates within the latter system, but the former principle is arbitrarily introduced in the "Live court show" to create the perception of a trial where "all will be treated fairly before the law" [1 ep. 1]. Indeed, the "Live court show" is presented as "a trial where justice stands" because "the entire nation will take part as members of the jury," as the show's promotional claims asserts: "Deliver justice with your ruling. A safe Korea is now about to get real." [1 ep. 1]. Thanks to the show, the devil judge creates the illusion of an accessible and fair trial by stripping it of technicalities. However, the trial is entirely in the judge's hands, who manipulates it by leveraging the emotions of the participating public.

The stated reason for launching the show is that trust in the judicial system is at an all-time low. In the real world, in 2022, OECD countries scored an average of 0.72 (out of 1) for freedom of civil justice from improper government influence, which influences citizens' trust in the judiciary, with Korea scoring around the mean at 0.71. Regarding affordability and access to civil justice, which is considered crucial for restoring trust in the judicial system and democracy, the OECD average is 0.65, with Korea scoring 0.70 [69]. No specific data are available for criminal justice, but it is assumed that citizens' trust in the judicial system is influenced by their direct experience with civil disputes, as these affect a larger majority of citizens than criminal cases. Contrary to the data above, another OECD study shows that only 33% of Korean citizens trust the courts and the judicial system [70], and during the Candlelight Protests, a survey identified "political independence and fairness of the prosecutor's office" as the most important reform issue according to respondents [20]. Indeed, distrust caused by improper government influence is a frequently explored topic in K-dramas, suggesting a widespread concern in public opinion. This phenomenon is not limited to Korea but is shared by many countries worldwide, where there is growing unease about declining trust in judicial systems. This does not mean that judicial systems are failing everywhere. What is failing is trust in society in general. Research on public trust in the justice system across 20 European countries indicates that trust is influenced not only by the system's functioning but also by citizens' satisfaction with their own lives and their trust in other people [71]. Other research shows that poor economic growth, social inequality, and a lack of upward social mobility cause a sense of powerlessness that affects people's trust in democracy, which is blamed for socio-economic inequality [17]. At the root of these trends is the perceived loss of socio-political agency [72].

The devil judge leverages these feelings, framing the trial and his role as an expression of the people's agency. He declares, "I am the power. And I will exercise jurisdiction entrusted to me by our people who are the sovereign power" [1 ep. 1]. Yet, his methods, even in a traditional trial context, are non-procedural. This is criticized as a crime by the second male protagonist, the devil judge's young assistant judge, who states, "It's a crime to use a trial as a tool" [1 ep. 5]. He firmly believes that "a judge is most powerful when he goes by the law" [1 ep. 7] and fears the nation endorsing the judge's unprocedural methods "as much as criminals" [1 ep. 5]. The young judge's mentor emphasizes this point, arguing that the devil judge's trial is "a trial of public opinion. Not a trial that goes by the principles of law" [1 ep. 6]. He condemns the devil judge for acting beyond his function, thus undermining judicial independence, which is necessary "for the nation to persist" [1 ep. 8]. Moreover, the devil judge's real goal is not societal or judicial reform. His ultimate aim is to exact revenge on the oligarchs who harmed the only people he ever loved. His plan is to use the live trial to manipulate public opinion and take down his enemies, one by one.

"Who does not have a situation? But not everyone is breaking the law" [1 ep. 5], deplores the paragon of honesty in the series, the police officer and young judge's sweetheart. Nevertheless, public opinion is captivated by the devil judge's charm, which he skillfully uses as he knows that "people tend to believe the words from someone who's charming, rather than someone who is right. In other words, charm is power" [1 ep. 1]. The public is also deceived by the (illusory) idea of regaining power against the elite through their participation in criminal rulings, as the judge cleverly selects trials that impeach the powerful. The series' viewers are similarly drawn in, not only by the judge's charismatic appearance but also by his vigilante-like behavior, for example, when he appears out of nowhere at night, like Batman, driving a Corvette just like Bruce Wayne, to punish an arrogant offspring of the oligarchy [1 ep. 2].

The devil judge is essentially an individual willing to exploit judicial power and manipulate the system to achieve his goals, prioritizing results over procedure. When he nearly turns the citizens into co-executioners of a death sentence, the young judge exposes the devil judge's unlawful deeds. The devil judge then admits that he has been "abusing the law" but justifies it by saying he did it "to punish criminals" in a society where "the law is silent in front of power" and because he "wanted to use whatever means to make them pay the price" [1 ep. 15]. Although he is admitting to his crimes, not out of guilt but as a new strategy, both fictional and real audiences can relate to his advocacy for justice. Moreover, fictional viewers can justify his actions and perceive realism in his behaviors, for they know about the traumas that he suffered because of the oligarchy, with the melodramatic mode amplifying sympathy and even empathy.

Judge-turned-writer Moon Yoo-seok notes that citizens' anger stems from "a system that has failed to operate properly" and that they "cannot come together in solidarity to solve issues." Nevertheless, he finds it "scary and sad how they come to rely on the outrageous measures taken by Yo-han [the devil judge]" [73]. "There is no easy justice in the world" [1 ep. 1, 12], claims the series, posing the fundamental question of whether we are willing to abandon a system—the rule of law and the separation of powers under democratic principles—that cost us blood to build, because it is not working as it should and due to our frustration. According to the screenwriter, "The genuine ending of the story" is the young judge's final line: "To make a world that does not need Yo-han, what should I do?" The young judge, who delivers the line, is one of the most unresolved characters in the series. Torn until the very end between the principles of the law and the reasoning of the devil judge, he ultimately decides to support his "fight against the distorted world" [1 ep. 8]. He finds his voice when he reproaches previous generations, embodying generational resentment: "You should have done a good job," he says to his mentor. "If people like you had done a good job … this would not have happened. People with such responsibilities should have done a better job" [1 ep. 8]. However, he is unable to find an independent way forward and thus also embodies his generation's disorientation. Once the devil judge leaves Korea, the young judge is left without guidance, and his final line reflects uncertainty about what to do next rather than confidence in his own abilities and the future. Viewers are also invited to reflect on the dystopian methods of the devil judge, and the final line leaves the series' ending and its central question open. From a narratological perspective, this is an ending that presents a problem without offering a viable solution, as the series portrays no successful alternative to the devil judge's unlawful and antisocial behavior. As a result, viewers are left with only an assessment of reality and their own powerlessness.

6. Vincenzo and the mobster myth

TDJ poses a further question that lies at the core of V as well: are we willing to follow charming leaders, no matter what they do, because democracy has weakened and state institutions have failed us? V is a dark comedy and the last installment of screenwriter Park Jae-beom's "justice trilogy" (*Good Manager* 2017, *The Fiery Priest* 2019). Combining sharp social criticism with satirical humor, the trilogy tells stories where justice is entrusted to figures unaffiliated with any state institution, delivering comedic shows "about the threats against justice writ large" [74]. The topics of leadership and the threats to justice in contemporary societies are addressed in V through the story of a Korean-born child raised in Italy, where he was adopted and given the name Vincenzo. There, he becomes a mob boss. When a feud within his clan forces him to flee, he returns to Korea to retrieve an enormous amount of gold hidden under a building in the Geumga Plaza in Seoul. As his plan clashes with a conglomerate's interest in building a high-rise tower in the area, a no-holds-barred conflict erupts between the malevolent conglomerate, Babel Group, aided by an ominous law firm, and the equally sinister mobster. Ultimately, Vincenzo gains the upper hand, as the final three episodes escalate into a bloody fight that culminates with the chaebol's lawyer being burned to death and the chaebol himself being killed after 24 hours of torture. In this conflict, Vincenzo finds himself allied with the tenants of Geumga Plaza, who are endangered by Babel's unlawful methods.

Like the devil judge, Vincenzo exudes an irresistible ambiguous charm; upon first seeing him, the tenants remark that he gives off the "eerie vibe" of a "handsome movie villain" [2 ep. 1]. Vincenzo is consistently depicted as an antihero. Antiheroes are main characters who lack conventional heroic attributes. They are morally gray rather than immoral and often resort to violence. Their surging popularity is a defining trend of contemporary TV fiction, at least in the US [75], and from there, they have become popular worldwide. Interpreted as embodiment of postmodernist moral relativism and the contradictions in contemporary society, antiheroes also "appear to be valued for their complexity, unconventionality, realism, and relatability" ([76], p. 173). Lastly, these narratives have been used by cable TV and streaming content providers as a market differentiation strategy compared to traditional and state TV, where morally unquestionable heroes are prevalent [77].

The antagonists of the antihero are portrayed as purebred villains, bad to the bone, perverse, ruthlessly abusive, and irredeemably corrupt, to the extent that the use of (excessive) violence and unlawful means to stop them seems reasonable. In TDJ and V, villains are members of the social elite who wield their hideous power against democratic institutions and the powerless. This framing follows the traditional melodramatic mode of K-dramas, but it is so overemphasized that the antiheroes' deviation from moral standards and societal norms is presented as justified, righteous, and even auspicious. "In times of turmoil a monster will appear" is said in TDJ [1 ep. 1]. Then the devil judge emerges and gains support from the honest and the oppressed. Similarly, in V, an "upright, old-fashioned lawyer" [2 ep. 5] wishes "a real monster could appear and deal with all these evil men, whether it is legal or not," and then asks the mobster if he can be that monster [2 ep. 3]. The powerless do not even want the mobster to redeem himself by "becoming a new person." They ask him to "do what you do best," which is to act as an outlaw because "that's what you can do to help the world" [2 ep. 16]. What emerges is that the non-abuse of force by the weak is not an ethical choice but the result of their lack of access to the power needed to avoid being wronged. This leads to delegating both the responsibility of the use of force and the burden associated with using illegal means to a morally questionable yet powerful third party, the antihero. Vincenzo's methods are considered "the lesser evil" [2 ep. 19]; however, he is consistently framed as a source of agency, understood as the social capacity to make autonomous choices, to exert influence independently of societal constraints, and to take moral responsibility for one's actions. The agency embodied by the titular character is articulated through the idealization of the mobster.

Let us be clear: Vincenzo has nothing to do with a real mobster. He is an ironic distillation of Hollywood clichés about the Italian charismatic mobster. Explicit intertextual references highlight the mythologization of the mobster, following the model of *The Godfather* [78]. This post-Hollywood mobster in K-drama style far surpasses the US model and is equated to an inspirer of social awareness and a charismatic leader of popular revolutions. First of all, Vincenzo shows relatable moral values: he does not mess with normal people [2 ep. 5], does not harm innocents [2 ep. 10], and takes his responsibility for "you have to pay the price for your actions" [2 ep. 8]. Driven by these values, his fight against the conglomerate shifts from a business endeavor to a personal vendetta when the powerful cross the line, making the battle "about the principle that [Vincenzo has] lived by." [2 ep. 10]. In the second place, when the plaza's tenants gather around him, he empowers them, as they say themselves: "All this time, we thought we were weak. But we were not weak. We just did not try to be strong." [2 ep. 17]. "We did not have a good reason to fight," but now they do "have a legitimate reason to fight," and the mobster is the one who gave it to them [2 ep. 19]. As a consequence, and this is the third step, they develop social awareness: "We've become interested in what's happening around us. We used not to care because we were busy making a living. Now it feels like it's our business" [2 ep. 15]; what they missed, and awaited, was "a strong leader" [2 ep. 11]. The most apologetic (and hilarious) of the mobster's supporters even says, "I finally realized why these people remained here and stood their ground. They were inspired by Vincenzo's strength and excellent leadership. That means that Vincenzo is not the Mafia. He's Che Guevara" [2 ep. 8]. Vincenzo brings to life a new social cohesion among the powerless who choose to act outside the law, knowing that the law cannot help them. Yet, "the law is not to blame," acknowledges Vincenzo: "It's all because of those bastards who deal with the law" [2 ep. 10]. He believes that the system cannot withstand the infringements of the ultra-powerful [2 ep. 10, 20], echoing the devil judge's words: "There is no way around it if those who dominate the world form a team" [1 ep. 11]. The only way around it is through the solidarity of the oppressed. That's why the tenants praise Vincenzo because he "got [them] together as a community" [2 ep. 19]. This is a mighty social message. Too bad, when the powerless form a team and become the antihero's sidekicks, they also become accomplice in his crimes.

The unsettling aspect of this dark satire is precisely the allegiance of the powerless with the antihero; laughing and joking, they get blood on their hands. Furthermore, there is a deceptive ambiguity not in the inherently questionable morality of the antiheroes but in how they become allies of the weak. In TDJ and V, the protagonists pursue their own agendas and end up functioning as a force for good because their interests coincidentally align with those of an oppressed. As a result, they take on a pro-social (heroic) behavior. At the end of the story, Vincenzo develops into a different kind of antihero, gaining an awareness of the pro-social effects of his actions as a villain. In his final lines, he states his new ethics: "I'm still a villain and could not care less about justice… One cannot win against any villain with justice alone. If merciless justice exists, I am willing to yield to it… I've taken up a new hobby: getting rid of garbage. If I do not do that, people will die buried underneath the garbage" [2 ep. 20]. This generates a fundamental shift in the character's portrayal. Let us first recollect the previous framing patterns: the melodramatic mode has been used to justify acts of violence because they are proportional to the conglomerate's hyper-vicious deeds. The antihero's extreme resort to violence is caused by Babel harming innocents and even killing his biological mother. The mother is the epitome of the melodramatic, pitiful victim. She had been presumed dead and had just reunited with her beloved son. Alone in the world, she was oppressed by abusive chaebols and wrongfully convicted. As a terminally ill cancer patient, she hopes for nothing more than to die in peace but is murdered while holding her son's picture because Babel wants to demonstrate its power over him. From here, the protagonist's fight turns into a dutiful vendetta, with the uncontroversial victimization of his mother projecting onto him as well. Furthermore, Vincenzo magnifies the trope of the charming criminal and undergoes a process of idealization, which is most likely to happen "for those characters whose ultimate motives or outcomes are perceived to be more heroic than villainous" ([76], p. 174). Finally, his leadership has reignited social unity among the oppressed, and he has received spiritual endorsement from a Buddhist monk: Vincenzo will never become pure, but he can still receive praise if he fights for others, becoming a force of equilibrium between good and evil in the world [2 ep. 20]. The series' final lines complete all of this, blurring the inherent individualism of the villain behind his "new hobby," thus shifting the framing from a forgivable and useful criminal to a pro-social villain.

This casts an enduring positive light on the antihero, extending his social usefulness beyond his accidental alliance with the powerless and changing the viewers' perspective, too. Regarding the latter, as the leading actor states, "The countries that love *Vincenzo* also experience the same societal issues that we critiqued in the show. I think they feel a sense of satisfaction" [79]. Yet, there is a tricky short circuit between the sense of satisfaction that a fictional representation can provide and its possible real-world implications. As RR states, if people want to see "the rich losing out," they "have no choice but to flock to the cinemas," "because it will never happen in reality" [4 ep. 3]. This satisfaction particularly enhances the popularity of the protagonist who is credited with having brought justice. Against the backdrop of this popularity, which can potentially influence viewers, as influence depends "upon viewers' levels of empathy for the main character in the drama" ([80], p. 211), I see the rising popularity of political leadership that is not constrained by democratic and legal frameworks. A World Values Survey proved that the number of citizens who would approve of a strong leader "who does not have to bother with parliament or elections" has risen since the turn of the century in most surveyed countries [81]. Furthermore, research addressing the relationship between viewers' antisocial tendencies and perceived affinity with antiheroes shows that viewers' "dark traits" lead them to consume content that reflects those tendencies [76]. This may have contributed to the success of streaming platforms' marketing strategy of distributing antihero narratives. It still cannot be ruled out that exposure to antiheroes "both reflects *and* exacerbates antisocial tendencies" ([76], p. 174) and has influence on political views and choices. It is fair to assume that media platforms' algorithms play a role in pushing forward similar content, thereby prolonging exposure to the same kind of narratives. This may lead to an equally prolonged suspension of counter-argument and enhance confirmation bias, which is the human tendency to look for information that confirms what one already thinks and not what challenges one's beliefs.

7. Can society be saved at all?

Vincenzo embodies a counterpower that becomes socially beneficial by curbing the crimes of a dysfunctional economic power represented by the chaebol, which is so mighty that it can exert control over politics, law enforcement, media, and the judiciary. The duel between the chaebol and the mobster erupts because state authorities are unable to control systemic imbalances. Another topic of the series is the social damage that corporate interests can cause. For example, Babel plans to produce painkillers containing opioids, opening the door to consumers' narcotic addiction "like in the States" [2 ep. 3]. The Korea-to-globe commensurability in this context is striking. While opioid overuse is a rising concern in Korea [82], the problem has already escalated in the US, where "opioid analgesics have been linked to the largest number of overdose deaths of any illicit drug class, outpacing those for cocaine and heroin combined" ([83], p. 25). By fueling debate on these topics, K-dramas seem to raise a troubling question: what if corporate crimes harming society are not the exception but the inevitable outcome of profit-seeking, inherent to "the very nature of what corporations are" ([84], p. 292)? K-dramas clearly find this hypothesis worth investigating, as the representation of corporate misconduct ranges from unethical behaviors and human rights violations to major criminal offenses. The most frequently represented corporate crimes include breach of fiduciary duty, embezzlement, tax evasion, misrepresentation of financial statements, stock market manipulation, money laundering, unfair competition, bid rigging, bribery, corruption, defamation, harassment, vexation, unfair dismissal, mobbing, media control, and manipulation of information. The large-scale effects of corporate conglomerate policies are also depicted, with common topics such as mass layoffs, anti-union policies, environmental damage, and nepotism. These issues are not merely products of popular imagination. Research shows that corporate crimes carry a heavier financial burden and have claimed more lives than street crimes.

Economic powers do not take all the blame, as political powers are equally responsible and consistently depicted as colluding with the money elite. "Nowadays, without money, you cannot be a leader," says the villain in AML. "Look at America," he adds. "If you don't know the economy, you can't have power. It's a time where money is power" [3 ep. 3]. The connivance between chaebols and politicians undermines trust more severely in the latter since the former is perceived as inherently selfish. "Do you know what democratization is?" says a first-generation chaebol in RR: "Before, only a single soldier was after the money in my pocket. That turned into three civilians" [4 ep. 2]. The chaebol equates the military dictator with the three presidential candidates of the 1987 democratic elections, sarcastically underscoring that every political system is equally willing to tap into economic power. The bottom line of K-dramas is that every political power is entangled in a symbiotic relationship with economic power, which undermines democracy and erodes public trust. This entanglement is a consequence of the historical relationship between governments and chaebols in Korea, as well as the inevitable connection between organized capital and the state in contemporary societies worldwide. As a result, public opinion and scholars are questioning the structural responsibilities of states in creating conditions that enable or allow corporate crimes since state-corporate symbiosis is considered crucial in the production of corporate crime [85]. In K-dramas, the symbiotic organism of chaebols and politics is depicted as a foreign entity in the body of the nation of ordinary citizens. As a consequence, the elite becomes an emblem of social divide in a neocolonial narrative, where a minority exploits the masses. This mirrors the global economic dynamics observable throughout the Global South, characterized by "a weakening or re-articulation of the legitimation functions of the state" ([86], p. 1313).

AML presents two possible alternatives to this situation, associated with the opposing life paths of the protagonist and his antagonist. However, both paths prove to be impossible, leaving room for a third, frightening scenario. The drama is a second-chance story of a young, "brave, warm-hearted, impartial, and honest prosecutor" [3 ep. 1] who is murdered while investigating the country's most powerful politician, called the "Kingmaker" because he is so mighty that he controls the presidency. The prosecutor is sent back in time by the Grim Reaper to better prepare for the fight against the Kingmaker. In the end, the prosecutor wins, but what makes this show worthwhile is how the prosecutor wins, the antagonist, and the ending.

The prosecutor's primary goal is to gain power because, as the series repeatedly states, justice without power is ineffective. Gaining power means making money, creating a support network, and infiltrating the enemy's environment. He succeeds in doing all of this because, when sent back to relive half of his life, he retains all the knowledge and memories of his first life and uses them to manipulate the present, including his enemies and allies. Not only does he know the future, but he also knows far more than any other character. The same occurs in RR, where the protagonist also disguises historical knowledge as intuition. Thanks to this unnatural competitive advantage, they change their allies' destinies for the better, trick and defeat their enemies, accumulate a fortune, and avoid twists of fate. Thus, the protagonists win because they are given an impossible head start, which is pretty much akin to cheating and leads to unethical and illegal behavior. None of them is a true antihero, but their methods are neither realistic nor blameless. As for AML, the evil deeds of the villain and the protagonist's charm and background stories trigger the usual melodramatic mechanisms. Yet, in each confrontation between the protagonist and antagonist, it is the latter who stands out for his social analysis, met only by the hero's almost pleonastic statements of moral superiority.

Although he is on the losing end of the melodramatic stereotype, the villain's backstory and pleas give voice to a society paradoxically resorting to an anti-democratic system to save democracy. A former committed prosecutor let down by the judiciary in the early democratic years of Korea, which was too weak to pursue justice against the powerful, he became a politician. By employing illegal measures, he gained control over state and economic powers with the aim of reforming the system by dominating it. Defying the principles of separation of powers, democratic processes, and the rule of law, he builds an autocratic occult regime in which every state power, as well as economic power, is subordinated to the common good, which is determined solely by the leader. This backstory is analogous to that of TDJ and V's most cunning enemies, who, much like in AML, are allies of the elite but not chaebols. These villains are wounded and disillusioned by a society that has failed them, so they decide to exploit its flaws to wield their personal power. In TDJ and V, this power serves the interests of the villains and the oligarchy, while in AML, it is intended to serve the common interest. AML's villain represents a counterpower that operates within the system and is driven by a sincere concern for the nation as well as by distrust in democracy's self-regulatory mechanisms, parliamentarism, and the party system. Claiming that he does not "think about anything else but how to make this country strong" [3 ep. 9], he severely reproaches politicians involved in scandals. Calling them sinners who fail the nation, he criticizes them for neglecting their responsibilities as people's representatives and leaders, while "for the nation to properly function, the politicians must come to their senses" [3 ep. 10]. When a chaebol threatens to resort to massive layoffs, he stops him, arguing that the national interest must take precedence over corporate interests [3 ep. 10]. He believes conflicts between political parties are the cause for the country "competitiveness is falling behind" [3 ep. 10]; therefore, he advocates for shared policies of social and economic growth.

The villain's autocratic dream of national unity and recovery under his occult leadership is doomed to fail thanks to the hero, who reaffirms the primacy of democratic law and institutions. However, the hero's path is also not entirely righteous, and above all, it is not feasible since it is made possible by superhuman powers. Most importantly, when the villain is defeated, his entourage and network of collusions do not dismantle but reorganize under a new leader, who is even worse than the previous one. While the former villain was righteous in intention but not in methods, the new one is a completely unrighteous head of a conglomerate with only personal greed and no interest in the common good. History repeats itself as political power is once again willingly subdued to an unlawful power, giving rise to a far worse alliance between economic power and state authorities, devoid of any semblance of national interest.

8. Conclusions

Korea's history since 1910 stands out as a condensation of the world history of the past three centuries, culminating in the apparent happy ending of its current status among the world's wealthiest nations. Korea's spectacular transformation and socio-economic growth seem almost like a fairy tale, as if Haiti could become Switzerland in less than five decades, as Chang puts it [8 p. xix]. However, while the nation justifiably takes pride in its economic miracle, it does not portray it as an achievement within Western universalist narratives of modernity, teleologically oriented around the notions of development, modernization, and progress. Rather, Korean popular representation of its recent memories questions the downsides of capitalism, particularly in the neoliberal age, offering a wide range of relatable topics to audiences in both the Global South and North. What emerges is that 40 years into neoliberalism have exacerbated economic and social inequalities inherent in the capitalist system, increasing class gaps, fragmentation, and decline in social trust, creating a new common ground of mutual understanding worldwide. Korean cultural productions' severe societal criticism addresses economic polarization and class antagonism between the political-economic elite and ordinary people, deteriorating living conditions, lack of social protection policies, violation of fair processes, corruption, and collusion.

The inherent transnationality of these topics, the exceptionally high quality of Korean audiovisual industry, the policies of the industry stakeholders targeting foreign audience and capital, and the favorable convergence of interests with the global content distribution market drive the success of K-dramas within the K-wave and determine its international influence [87]. Moreover, the audience's unfamiliarity with Korean history facilitates the decontextualized interpretation and generalization of K-drama content, thereby enhancing its global relatability and localization. In other words, the story's exemplarity emerges, making the message relatable across time and space, while the loss of information does not impoverish the essence of the message. For example, in recent Korean debates targeting the monopolistic chaebol system, chaebol reform has "become synonymous with the concept of economic democracy" ([88], p. 395). The global audience may be unaware that the concept of a state acting to "democratize the economy" was incorporated into the Korean Constitution in 1987, when Korea transitioned out of dictatorship (Article 119–2). While the audience may miss the nuances of the debate on the state's limits in granting a constitutional right or managing national economy [89], it is abundantly clear that the topic permeating K-dramas, although simplified, is the need for a solution to the "monopolization of power by socioeconomic groups, such as chaebol, and by the wider capitalist class" ([88], p. 409). The audience may also not realize that chaebols are family-owned conglomerates with a very specific historical relationship with local political regimes, nor may they consider the managerial disadvantages of a family-led conglomerate in the contemporary market. Yet, the strength of these chaebol narratives is precisely that chaebols are families. They have a face: they are not identity-less financial powers but characters with human interactions, their own (im)morality, kinship, and feelings. In short, it is much easier for the public to relate to them and grasp the essence of the social criticism conveyed through their narratives. A recent K-drama that attempts to draw a detailed picture of Korean economic history is RR; hence, it is less understandable to viewers. As a result, it compensates for the script's complex technicalities by heavily leveraging stereotypes of the "blinded by greed" chaebols [4 ep. 1], who are already well-known among viewers as a target of K-dramas' criticism, with their misconducts sarcastically referred to as "an occupational disease" [4 ep. 6].

My argument, toward the conclusion, is that K-dramas translate the perception that society is becoming increasingly unjust on different levels into narratives where the concept of justice, expressed through judicial cases, takes the foreground and is tackled by addressing the responsibilities of specific institutions, social bodies, and powers. K-drama's melodramatic mode is revived in these narratives, guiding the viewer's response to condemn major value violations and empathize with those who suffer injustice, typically the powerless. Lines such as "Why are the powerless citizens the only ones suffering? This is not justice" [4 ep. 6] could fit in any drama and could be uttered by any non-elite character. However, more than the pursuit of justice, contemporary Korean narratives brilliantly portray the desire for revenge disguised as justice and the deceitfulness of a revenge that "is not for those who have been wronged" but is the prerogative of those "with power." [4 ep. 16].

The case studies represent narratives that, departing from a critical portrayal of contemporary society, heighten belief in the justifiability of unlawful or out-of-system reactions to the unfairness of society. By translating global citizens' feelings of impotence, having lost their social and political agency [72], these K-dramas envision alternatives, but the reappropriation of agency is achieved through twisted leadership. Indeed, salvation from unjust powers for ordinary people comes via redeemers from the upper class (TDJ), or equipped with anti-social and harmful powers (V), or gifted with unrealistic second chances, or operating on the fringes of legality (AML, RR). Justice is served by the grace of extraordinary (male) protagonists and through illicit, illegal, morally disputable actions. In the struggle against overwhelming unbalances, the only alternative left seems to be rebellion under the questionable authority of a charming dark leader. As in dystopian narratives, these series "heightened subjects' openness to radical political action—without activating them politically in more conventional ways." Hence, they expand the political imagination of viewers "outside the normal realm of democratic politics" ([90], p. 983). Rather than fostering delusional hope in the future as an improvement, these narratives mirror the helplessness of the lower classes, their inability to achieve justice and equality for themselves without an external source of power, and the risks of this. Moreover, the redeemer is often someone greatly offended by the higher classes. Thus, it is not his inner uprightness that drives him to embrace the cause of social justice. Friends or foes, either way, in the end, the fate of the lower classes seems to be in someone else's hands.

Thanks

I would like to thank the anonymous reviewers for helping me improve this chapter and Professor Giammarco Sigismondi for his precious advices. I also extend my gratitude to Professor Han Taejun, President of Ghent University Global Campus, as well as my colleagues, our beloved students, and all the people I met in South Korea, for aiding me in better understanding Korean society and culture.

Author details

Mara Santi
Ghent University, Ghent, Belgium

*Address all correspondence to: mara.santi@ugent.be

IntechOpen

© 2024 The Author(s). Licensee IntechOpen. This chapter is distributed under the terms of the Creative Commons Attribution License (http://creativecommons.org/licenses/by/4.0), which permits unrestricted use, distribution, and reproduction in any medium, provided the original work is properly cited.

References

[1] Choi J. The Devil Judge [Television Series]. Seoul: tvN; 2021. 16 episodes

[2] Kim H. Vincenzo [Television Series]. Seoul: tvN; 2021. 20 episodes

[3] Han C, Kim Y. Again my Life [Television Series]. Seoul: SBS; 2022. 16 episodes

[4] Jeong D. Reborn Rich [Television Series]. Seoul: JTBC. Aired; 2022. 16 episodes

[5] Pacheco PR. Shrimp to Whale. South Korea from the Forgotten War to K-Pop. Vol. xix. London: Hurst & Co.; 2022. 315 p

[6] Ringen S, Kwon H, Yi I, Kim T, Lee J. Korean State and Social Policy: How South Korea Lifted itself from Poverty and Dictatorship to Affluence and Democracy. Oxford: Oxford UP; 2011. DOI: 10.1093/acprof: oso/9780199734351.001.0001. 146 p

[7] Kim BK, Vogel EF. The Park Chung Hee Era. The Transformation of South Korea. Cambridge MI: Harvard UP; 2013. 744 p

[8] Chang HJ. Bad Samaritans. The Myth of Free Trade and the Secret History of Capitalism. Vol. xxv. New York: Bloomsbury Press; 2007. 254 p

[9] Kang DC. Crony Capitalism. Corruption and Development in South Korea and the Philippines. Cambridge: Cambridge UP; 2002. p. xvi. 204 p. DOI: 10.1017/CBO9780511606175

[10] Hamdani A, Kosenko K, Yishay Y. Regulatory measures to dismantle pyramidal business groups: Evidence from the United States, Japan, Korea and Israel. ECGI Law Working Paper [Internet]. 2020;**542**:1-36. Available from: https://ssrn.com/abstract=3692970 [Accessed: August 4, 2024]

[11] Global Soft Power Index. Nation Results. Brand Finance [Internet]. 2024. Available from: https://brandirectory.com/softpower/nation?country=75 [Accessed: August 4, 2024]

[12] Hofstede G, Hofstede GJ, Minkov M. Cultures and Organizations: Software of the Mind. Intercultural Cooperation and its Importance for Survival. 3rd ed. Vol. xiv. New York. London: McGraw-Hill; 2010. 576 p

[13] Country Comparison Tool. The Culture Factor Group [Internet]. 2023. Available from: https://www.hofstede-insights.com/country-comparison-tool?countries=south+korea [Accessed: August 4, 2024]

[14] The Economist's Glass-Ceiling Index. The Economist Group [Internet]. 2024. Available from: https://www.economist.com/graphic-detail/glass-ceiling-index [Accessed: August 4, 2024]

[15] Query: Causes of Mortality. Reference Area: Korea. Cause of Death: Intentional Self-Harm. Time Period: Start 2000. OECD Data Explorer [Internet]. Available from: https://data-explorer.oecd.org [Accessed: August 4, 2024]

[16] Jang H, Lee W, Kim Y, Kim H. Suicide rate and social environment characteristics in South Korea: The roles of socioeconomic, demographic, urbanicity, general health behaviors, and other environmental factors on suicide rate. BMC Public Health

[17] Houle C, Miller MK. Social mobility and democratic attitudes: Evidence from Latin America and sub-Saharan Africa. Comparative Political Studies. 2019;**52**(11):1610-1647. DOI: 10.1177/0010414019830719

[18] Amoranto G, Chun N, Deolalikar A. Who are the middle class and what values do they hold? Evidence from the world values survey. ADB Economics Working Paper Series [Internet]. 2010;**229**:1-20. Available from: http://hdl.handle.net/11540/1566 [Accessed: August 4, 2024]

[19] Clark C. The paradoxes in globalization's economic empowerment of South Korea. Korean Journal. 2015;**55**:31-58. DOI: 10.25024/kj.2015.55.1.31

[20] Lee Y. Articulating inequality in the candlelight protest of 2016-2017. Korean Journal. 2019;**59**(1):16-45. DOI: 10.25024/kj.2019.59.1.16

[21] Hacker JS, Pierson P. Winner-Take-all Politics. How Washington Made the Rich Richer and Turned its Back on the Middle Class. New York: Simon & Schuster; 2010. 357 p

[22] Park HO. Segyehwa: Globalization and nationalism in Korea. Journal of International Institute [Internet]. 1996;**4**(1). Available from: http://hdl.handle.net/2027/spo.4750978.0004.105 [Accessed: August 4, 2024]

[23] Najjar F. The Arabs, Islam and globalization. Middle East Policy. 2005;**12**:91-106. DOI: 10.1111/j.1061-1924.2005.00215.x

[24] Chua BH, Iwabuchi K, editors. East Asian Pop Culture. Analysing the Korean Wave. Vol. xi. 307 p. Hong Kong: Hong Kong UP; 2008. DOI: 10.5790/hongkong/9789622098923.001.0001

[25] Kim DK, Kim MS, editors. Hallyu. Influence of Korean Popular Culture in Asia and beyond. Seoul: Seoul National UP; 2011. 504 p

[26] Kim Y, editor. The Korean Wave. Korean Media Go Global. Vol. xvi, 233 p. London: Routledge; 2013. DOI: 10.4324/9781315859064

[27] Kuwahara Y. The Korean Wave. Korean Popular Culture in Global Context. Vol. ix, 243 p. New York: Palgrave Macmillan; 2014. DOI: 10.1057/9781137350282

[28] Lee S, Nornes AM. Hallyu 2.0. The Korean Wave in the Age of Social Media. Vol. vi, 268 p. Ann Arbor: University of Michigan Press; 2015. DOI: 10.3998/mpub.7651262

[29] Jin DY. New Korean wave. In: Transnational Cultural Power in the Age of Social Media. Urbana: University of Illinois Press; 2016. 232 p. DOI: 10.5406/illinois/9780252039973.001.0001

[30] Jin DY, Yoon K, Min W, Transnational hallyu. The Globalization of Korean Digital and Popular Culture. Vol. vii. London: Rowman & Littlefield; 2021, 188 p

[31] Kim Y. The soft power of the Korean wave. In: Parasite, BTS and Drama. Vol. xiv, 237 p. London: Routledge; 2022. DOI: 10.4324/9781003102489

[32] Oh DC, Han BM, editors. Korean Pop Culture beyond Asia. Race and Reception. Seattle: University of Washington Press; 2024. 290 p

[33] Kim T. K-culture without "K-"? The paradoxical nature of producing

Korean television towards a sustainable Korean wave. The International Journal of Communication-US [Internet]. 2023;**17**:149-170. Available from: http://ijoc.org [Accessed: August 4, 2024]

[34] Ju H. The Korean wave and Korean dramas. In: Oxford Research Encyclopedia of Communication. Oxford: Oxford University Press; 2018. DOI: 10.1093/acrefore/9780190228613.013.715

[35] Jin DY. Theorizing the Korean wave. Introduction to new perspectives. The International Journal of Communication-US [Internet]. 2023;**17**:1-8. Available from: http://ijoc.org [Accessed: August 4, 2024]

[36] Jang G, Paik W. Korean wave as tool for Korea's new cultural diplomacy. Advances in Applied Sociology. 2012;**2**:196-202. DOI: 10.4236/aasoci.2012.23026

[37] Jin DY. An analysis of the Korean wave as transnational popular culture: North American youth engage through social media as TV becomes obsolete. The International Journal of Communication-US [Internet]. 2018;**12**:404-422. Available from: http://ijoc.org [Accessed: August 4, 2024]

[38] Baldacchino JP. In sickness and in love? Autumn in my heart and the embodiment of morality in Korean television drama. Korean Journal. 2014;**54**(4):5-28. DOI: 10.25024/kj.2014.54.4.5

[39] Kim D. Media Governance in Korea 1980-2017. Vol. xviii, 219 p. Cham: Palgrave Macmillan; 2018. DOI: 10.1007/978-3-319-70302-2

[40] Lotz A. In between the global and the local: Mapping the geographies of Netflix as a multinational service. International Journal of Cultural Studies. 2020;**24**(2):195-215. DOI: 10.1177/1367877920953166

[41] Second Quarter Earnings. Netflix [Internet]. 2024. Available from: https://s22.q4cdn.com/959853165/files/doc_financials/2024/q2/FINAL-Q2-24-Shareholder-Letter.pdf [Accessed: August 4, 2024]

[42] Durrani A. Top Streaming Statistics in 2024. Fobes Home [Internet]. 2024. Available from: https://www.forbes.com/home-improvement/internet/streaming-stats [Accessed: August 4, 2024]

[43] Kim KA, Park JH, Yoon S, Wang Y, Bae H, Luc KT. Duality of K-content in the era of Netflix: An investigation of Korean "Netflix original" characteristics. International Journal of Communication-US [Internet]. 2023;**17**:7015-7039. Available from: http://ijoc.org [Accessed: August 4, 2024]

[44] Park S, Hong SK. Reshaping Hallyu: Global reception of South Korean content on Netflix. International Journal of Communication-US [Internet]. 2023;**17**:6952-6971. Available from: http://ijoc.org [Accessed: August 4, 2024]

[45] Jin DY. Transnational proximity and universality in Korean culture: Analysis of squid game and BTS. Seoul Journal of Korean Studies. 2022;**35**(1):5-28. DOI: 10.1353/seo.2022.0002

[46] What We Watched the Second Half of 2023. Netflix [Internet]. 2023. Available from: https://about.netflix.com/en/news/what-we-watched-the-second-half-of-2023 [Accessed: August 4, 2024]

[47] Park JH, Kim KA, Lee Y. Netflix and platform imperialism: How Netflix alters the ecology of the Korean TV drama industry. International Journal

of Communication-US [Internet]. 2023;**17**:72-91. Available from: http://ijoc.org [Accessed: August 4, 2024]

[48] Kim T. Cultural politics of Netflix in local contexts: A case of the Korean media industries. Media, Culture and Society. 2022;**44**(8):1508-1522. DOI: 10.1177/01634437221111917

[49] Delgado S. 17 daebak K-Dramas to get Obsessed With Right Now. From Romances to Sci-Fi Thrillers and Everything in Between. Tudum by Netflix [Internet]. 2024. Available from: https://www.netflix.com/tudum/articles/kdramas-on-netflix [Accessed: August 4, 2024]

[50] Jiang Z. Research on the strategic positioning of the Korean mainstream film and television market based on Netflix platform. In: SHS Web Conferences. International Conference on Digital Economy and Business Administration [Internet]. Vol. 181. Les Ulis: EDP Sciences; 2024. DOI: 10.1051/shsconf/202418104010

[51] Jin DY. Ten myths about the Korean wave in the global cultural sphere. International Journal of Communication-US [Internet]. 2021;**15**:4147-4164. Available from: http://ijoc.org [Accessed: August 4, 2024]

[52] We JY. Melodramatic tactics for survival in the neoliberal era: Excess and justice in *the heirs* and *my love from the star*. The Journal of Korean Studies. 2018;**23**(1):153-173. DOI: 10.1215/21581665-4339098

[53] Abelmann N. The Melodrama of Mobility. Women, Talk, and Class in Contemporary South Korea. Vol. xviii, 325 p. Honolulu: University of Hawaii Press; 2003. DOI: 10.21313/9780824864859

[54] Yuan Y. Third-space K-drama: Netflix, Hallyu, and the melodramatic mundane. International Journal of Communication-US [Internet]. 2023;**17**:6990-7014. Available from: http://ijoc.org [Accessed: August 4, 2024]

[55] Ju H. Korean TV drama viewership on Netflix: Transcultural affection, romance, and identities. Journal of International and Intercultural Communication. 2019;**13**(1):32-48. DOI: 10.1080/17513057.2019.1606269

[56] Park Y. From the era of melodrama to the age of the comedy. The simultaneous transformations of Korean society and film genre from the 1990s to the present. Korean Journal. 2019;**59**(4):103-135. DOI: 10.25024/kj.2019.59.4.103

[57] Kim S. (In)commensurability of Korean cinema: International coproduction of Korean films in the 2010s. Korean Journal. 2019;**59**(4):136-166. DOI: 10.25024/kj.2019.59.4.136

[58] Baldacchino JP, Park EJ. Between fantasy and realism. Gender, identification and desire among Korean viewers of second-wave Korean dramas. European Journal of East Asian Studies. 2020;**20**(2):285-309. DOI: 10.1163/15700615-20211002

[59] Anker ER. Orgies of Feeling: Melodrama and the Politics of Freedom. Vol. xiv, 338 p. Durham: Duke UP; 2014. DOI: 10.1215/9780822376545

[60] Jin DY. Transnational proximity of the Korean wave in the global cultural sphere. International Journal of Communication-US [Internet]. 2023;**17**:9-28. Available from: http://ijoc.org [Accessed: August 4, 2024]

[61] Innocenti V, Pescatore G. Changing series: Narrative models and the role of the viewer in contemporary

television seriality. Between [Internet]. 2014;**4**(8):1-15. Available from: https://ojs.unica.it/index.php/between/article/view/4 [Accessed: August 4, 2024]

[62] Zunshine L. Why we read fiction. In: Theory of Mind and the Novel. Vol. x. Columbus: Ohio State UP; 2006, 198 p

[63] Zunshine L. Getting inside your Head. What Cognitive Science Can Tell us about Popular Culture. Vol. xiii. Baltimore: The Johns Hopkins UP; 2012, 217 p

[64] Igartua JJ. Identification with characters and narrative persuasion through fictional feature films. Communications. 2010;**35**:347-373. DOI: 10.1515/comm.2010.019

[65] Yuan Y, Major-Girardin J, Brown S. Storytelling is intrinsically mentalistic: A functional magnetic resonance imaging study of narrative production across modalities. Journal of Cognitive Neuroscience. 2018;**30**(9):1298-1314. DOI: 10.1162/jocn_a_01294

[66] Kaplan JT et al. Processing narratives concerning protected values: A cross-cultural investigation of neural correlates. Cerebral Cortex. 2017;**27**(2):1428-1438. DOI: 10.1093/cercor/bhv325

[67] Cho H, Shen L, Wilson K. Perceived realism: Dimensions and roles in narrative persuasion. Communication Research. 2014;**41**(6):828-851. DOI: 10.1177/0093650212450585

[68] Yang H, editor. Law and Society in Korea. Vol. xvii. Cheltenham: Edward Elgar; 2013, 236 p

[69] Access to Justice. OECD [Internet]. Available from: https://www.oecd.org/en/topics/access-to-justice.html [Accessed: August 4, 2024]

[70] OECD. OECD Survey on Drivers of Trust in Public Institutions 2024 Results. Korea [Internet]: Country notes; 2024. Available from: https://www.oecd.org/en/publications/oecd-survey-on-drivers-of-trust-in-public-institutions-2024-results-country-notes_a8004759-en/korea_ab1a95c7-en.html [Accessed: August 4, 2024]

[71] Van de Walle S. Trust in the justice system: A comparative view across Europe. Prison Service Journal. 2009;**183**:22-26

[72] Bauman Z. In Search of Politics. Vol. vi. Stanford: Stanford UP; 1999, 212 p

[73] Lee G. The Devil Judge' Writer Moon Yoo-Seok Shares Creating Dystopian Society. Seoul: The Korea Times [Internet]; 2021. Available from: https://www.koreatimes.co.kr/www/art/2024/07/398_315543.html [Accessed: August 4, 2024]

[74] Yun S. Architects of K-Dramas. Jeju-do: Koreana [Internet]; 2022. Available from: https://www.koreana.or.kr/koreana/na/ntt/selectNttInfo.do?nttSn=115932&bbsId=1114 [Accessed: August 4, 2024]

[75] Vaage MB. The Antihero in American Television. Vol. xxii. New York: Routledge; 2016. p. 216

[76] Greenwood D, Ribieras A, Clifton A. The dark side of antiheroes: Antisocial tendencies and affinity for morally ambiguous characters. Psychology of Popular Media. 2020;**10**(2):165-177. DOI: 10.1037/ppm0000334

[77] García AN. Moral emotions, antiheroes and the limits of allegiance. In: García AN, editor. Emotions in Contemporary TV Series. London: Palgrave Macmillan; 2016. pp. 52-70. DOI: 10.1007/978-1-137-56885-4_4

[78] Larke-Walsh GS. Screening the Mafia. Masculinity, Ethnicity and Mobsters from the Godfather to the Sopranos. Vol. v. Jefferson: McFarland; 2010, 282 p

[79] Loh L. Exclusive: Vincenzo star Song Joong-ki talks to Tatler about the Netflix hit. Tatler [Internet]. 2021. Available from: https://www.tatlerasia.com/lifestyle/entertainment/hk-tatler-exclusive-song-joong-ki-vincenzo-cassano-netflix [Accessed: August 4, 2024]

[80] Mutz DC, Nir L. Not necessarily the news: Does fictional television influence real-world policy preferences? Mass Communication and Society. 2010;**13**(2):196-217. DOI: 10.1080/15205430902813856

[81] Foa R, Yascha M. The signs of deconsolidation. Journal of Democracy. 2017;**28**(1):5-16. DOI: 10.1353/jod.2017.0000

[82] Nahm FS. Increasing opioid prescription in Korea: A pressing public health concern and necessitating initiatives. The Korean Journal of Pain. 2024;**37**:1-2. DOI: 10.3344/kjp.23349

[83] National Drug Threat Assessment. United States Drug Enforcement Administration [Internet]. Washington DC: National Drug Threat Assessment; 2017. Available from: https://www.dea.gov/sites/default/files/2018-07/DIR-040-17_2017-NDTA.pdf [Accessed: August 4, 2024]

[84] Alcadipani R, Rodrigues C, Medeiros O. When corporations cause harm: A critical view of corporate social irresponsibility and corporate crimes. Journal of Business Ethics. 2020;**167**(2):285-297. DOI: 10.1007/s10551-019-04157-0

[85] Whyte D. Regimes of permission and state-corporate crime. State Crime Journal. 2014;**3**(2):237-246. DOI: 10.13169/statecrime.3.2.0237

[86] Ciocchini P, Greener J. Regimes of extreme permission in Southeast Asia: Theorizing state-corporate crime in the global south. The British Journal of Criminology. 2023;**63**(5):1309-1326. DOI: 10.1093/bjc/azac091

[87] Ju H. Transnational Korean Television. Cultural Storytelling and Digital Audiences. Vol. vii. Lanham: Lexington Books; 2020, 131 p

[88] Doucette J. Debating economic democracy in South Korea: The cost of commensurability. Critical Asian Studies. 2015;**47**(3):388-413. DOI: 10.1080/14672715.2015.1057025

[89] Lee JY. Neoliberal developmentalism in South Korea and the unfulfilled promise of economic and social rights. In: MacNaughton G, Frey DF, editors. Economic and Social Rights in a Neoliberal World. Cambridge: Cambridge UP; 2018. pp. 261-282

[90] Jones CW, Paris C. It's the end of the world and they know it: How dystopian fiction shapes political attitudes. Perspectives on Politics. 2018;**16**(4):969-989. DOI: 10.1017/S1537592718002153